TRAUMA-INFORMED DESIGN

A Framework for Designers, Architects, and Other Practitioners

First Edition

Christine Ann Awad Cowart, Janet E. Roche, Adrienne Erdman, and Dr. J. Davis Harte

Book design, cover, and infographics by Corin Hirsch.

Illustrations of domain applications by Architecture for Public Benefit.

ISBN: 979-8-218-52512-5
Second printing | February 2025

Praise for Trauma-informed Design

Working with the Trauma-informed Design Society for many years now, has been a great privilege and honor. This book is the culmination of so much of their wonderful work and answers many of the questions around what this means when it gets into practice and what we need to do to design effectively. This book is groundbreaking and a major advancement for the field of trauma-informed design.

> — *Erin Peavey, Vice President and Health and Well-being Design Leader, HKS*

Trauma-informed Design: A Framework for Designers, Architects, and Other Practitioners provided the ideal balance of academic background and practical instruction for architects to incorporate TiD principles throughout the spectrum of their work. *Trauma-informed Design* provides guidance for supporting clients with specific TiD requirements, as well as fundamentals for inclusion in all design projects.

> —*Graham Vickers, Senior Principle, Principal in Charge of Marketing, Director of Justice Practice, SMRT Architecture*

Finally! An innovative effort to address the critical importance of environment on supporting calming and healing potential within the population using the space. TiD provides ground breaking guidance for practitioners to create environments which integrate and leverage structural design processes with healing and resiliency concepts.

> —*Kim Bushey, Director of Correctional Risk Intervention Services*

This book will be a useful, foundational, and important tool for all disciplines who are part of a project from the earliest stages of concept to move in and beyond.
—*Mary Jo Cooper, Vice President of Developmental Services, Bay Cove Human Services*

As a social worker, school counselor, and educator, I highly recommend this book as an invaluable resource that demonstrates how personal trauma responses are connected to and affected by the environments in which we live and work. It clearly and seamlessly explains the importance and benefit of using trauma-informed design in our schools, especially as we see growing numbers of students affected by all levels of trauma. In many cases, the physical environment in which our children learn is the last consideration of our education system. This book explains how the converse is true and cites research showing why the design of the environment should be the first consideration. Using SAMHSA's key principles, you will learn how to effect positive change through using choice, comfort, movement, and play, as well as other principles, in school and classroom environments. This book should be required reading for every professional working in education.
—*Nancy Barber, MS Ed, LICSW*

DEDICATIONS

To my two dear sons, Moisés and Joaquín, who set me on the journey of a lifetime when they joined our family. It was through their bravery that I finally began to understand the world around me, including how trauma impacts each and every one of us. It was through their selflessness that I have been able to devote all my "free time" to helping others apply this understanding to heal, support one another, and design safe, stress-reducing, restorative spaces.

To my loving husband, Tony, whose ever-supporting nature and profound love have allowed me to immerse myself in my passion, fully assured that our family was well-tended. He has been my touch-stone for over 20 years, and I am forever thankful to have him as my confidant and advisor.

To Davis and Adrienne, my ever-patient instructors in the worlds of design and research, and Janet, the visionary behind the Trauma-informed Design Society, who opened my eyes to the impact of the physical environment.

To my parents, Guergues and Hannelore Awad, who demonstrated a work ethic unlike any other, and provided me with a strong foundation. I am thankful every day to have been buoyed by my Dad's insistence that I could shatter any glass ceiling, so I never stopped to question my path or whether I belonged. I am grateful to share his strong desire to understand the meanings and actions of others, and to serve where I can.

—Christine Ann Awad Cowart

To my Dad and my Mom, who taught me the importance of understanding, sympathy, empathy, and providing dignity to others, which has guided me through my entire life.

To my co-writers, Adrienne and Davis, I'm so humbled by your willingness to believe in this project.

And finally, to my co-pilot in this journey, Christine, for whom all my dreams and thoughts were just that, without you.

—Janet E. Roche

DEDICATIONS

To Christian, my marital best friend, for your unwavering encouragement and quiet strength. You have grounded me, made me feel safe and loved, and inspired me to love life. Your constant question, "How can I help?" is the gift that allowed me to reclaim myself and follow my passions.

To Reed and Graham, my beloved sons. You are my reason and my joy. Thank you for teaching me the importance of embracing each day with playfulness and wonder, and for inspiring me to create a world of safety and light.

To Janet, Christine, and Davis, my colleagues and friends, for your belief in me, for offering your trust and friendship, and for inviting me into your lives and journeys. I am stronger because of your support.

And to everyone who has experienced trauma yet continues to grow, learn, and rediscover their strength—May this book serve as a reminder of your resilience and a source of compassion as we work together to design spaces that heal.

—Adrienne Erdman

It is not I that accomplish these works but rather my higher self as I get out of the way. To my whole family, especially Michael and Freya, who uplift, support and help me grow every day. To my ancestors, I am nothing without you. To mama Earth and all the beings of planet Earth. Thank you for your true love. To those who paved the path before us; those visionary giants who lift us up with their timeless design-behavior research. To my colleagues, co-collaborators and the many others in this scholarly dialogue-adventure. Thank you for your sincere work. We are in this together. Thank you to all who read this book and strive to apply the ideas to practice. And most of all, this work is dedicated to the children. May you one day tell your grandchildren about a long-forgotten phenomenon of ACEs, as healing overtakes pain.

—Dr. J. Davis Harte

TABLE OF CONTENTS

PREFACE

THE CONCEPT OF TRAUMA-INFORMED DESIGN (TID) IS EMERGING AS we issue this resource. Trauma-informed Design Society cofounders Dr. J. Davis Harte and Janet Roche first encountered the term in 2016, while working and studying in the Boston Architectural College's Design for Human Health Master's Program. At the time, there was very little information available about this new concept, but some designers were starting to think about how they could use their knowledge of the impacts of the physical environment on human emotions to support individuals who had experienced trauma. Jill Pable and ShopWorks Architecture were on the forefront of applying these concepts to housing solutions for those experiencing homelessness.

Davis and Janet were drawn to the idea of designing physical spaces to support healing, and dove headlong into finding likeminded designers and compile resources on the subject. In 2019, Janet met Christine Cowart, who was focused on studying the impacts of trauma and trauma-informed care best practices, and introduced her to the concept of TiD. By 2020, Davis co-authored the "Design As the Missing Variable in Trauma-Informed Schools" chapter in E.Rossen's *Supporting and Educating Traumatized Students. A Guide for School-Based Professionals*. Later that year, the trio founded the Trauma-informed Design Society as a multidisciplinary team dedicated to learning and sharing information about TiD.

The Society's focus has grown, and now it is to develop a deep understanding of the latest research in the fields of trauma, neuroscience, therapeutic practices, architecture, and design, and use that understanding to identify ways through which design can support survivors of traumatic experiences. To this end, the Society is continually seeking out the latest studies, conducting research, applying the findings to practice, and then evaluating the outcomes, in a iterative feedback loop.

In support of these efforts, the Society formed a research team in 2023, comprised of professionals from related fields interested in the intersection between trauma-informed care and design. Adrienne Erdman, a member of the Research Team and one of the co-authors of this book, joined the TiD Society leadership team as Vice President of Research and Development in 2024.

Located across the United States (US), the Trauma-informed Design Society merges the co-founders' extensive experience in human services and interior design with the rapidly evolving field of trauma science, to help organizations implement a trauma-informed approach in their services and mitigate potential triggers and other stressors in the built environment. The Society is committed to ensuring that TiD practitioners have access to the latest research and resources so they can apply TiD to their projects with fidelity.

To reach this goal, the TiD Society operates in four main areas:

 * Researching TiD principles and practices, conducting studies to demonstrate their effectiveness, and compiling resources for practitioners;
 * Developing a standard for the provision of safe, effective, evidence-based TiD services;
 * Cultivating and providing rewarding professional development opportunities for TiD practitioners; and
 * Providing direct trauma-informed care and design project consultation services through sister organizations.

As TiD practitioners ourselves, we recognize that the people who we serve often represent vulnerable populations and marginalized communities. As such, we strongly believe that it is imperative that those who engage in this work not cause further harm, intentionally or otherwise. The TiD Framework set forth in these pages provides practitioners with the tools to engage in this work faithfully, and aligned with best practices, so they can protect against harm to their staff, clients, and others.

This work is based on our research and experience, as well as information gathered from countless architects and designers throughout the world. Some have been applying a trauma-informed approach to their work for many years, while others are just beginning to enter this area of practice. Each of these conversations has been immensely helpful in developing the TiD Framework, and we would be remiss if we did not mention the following practitioners who are standouts in the field: Kerri Brady, Alina Osnaga, Erin Peavey, Laura Rossbert, Graham Vickers, and Jennifer Wilson.

This book would not have been possible without the contributions provided by each member of the TiD Society's Research Team. They have dedicated countless hours to our efforts and the refinement of our approach. We are incredibly grateful to:

- * Evon Calabrese, EDAC, an architectural designer with a focus on evidence-based design;
- * Sarah Erdman Jordan, a licensed professional counselor and co-owner of Soul Haven Counseling;
- * Margie McNally, NCIDQ, LEED AP, CAPS, a designer with over 20 years of experience and focus on environmental design and lighting technology;
- * Heidi Niebauer, a disability, mental health, and housing advocate;
- * Molly Pierce, a pediatric occupational therapist with over 35 years of experience who works in public schools and as a consultant;
- * Cherry Price, a trauma-informed educator and consultant with over 27 years of experience; and
- * Krishna Sreenivas, an architect and designer, who worked in India for 15 years before relocating to the United States.

Each used their unique lens to share invaluable insights from their specific area of expertise. We are deeply appreciative of their support, assistance, and encouragement.

Prior to publishing, we reached out to some trusted advisors in various fields who are applying a trauma-informed approach to their work, and asked them to review the book and provide honest feedback. This team was comprised of some of our biggest cheerleaders, who are also consummate professionals we trust to tell us when we are on the wrong track. The feedback we received helped us ensure a comprehensive and indispensable final product. We therefore extend our thanks to:

- * Nancy Barber, LICSW, a clinical social worker, therapist, and educator currently serving as a school counselor for middle school students;
- * Kim Bushey, a director of correctional risk intervention services;
- * Mary Jo Cooper, a director of residential, family, and community developmental disability services at a human services agency and faculty member at an architectural college;
- * Alina Osnaga, an empirical sciences researcher and architectural designer focused on human-centered design;
- * Erin Peavey, an architect, researcher, and advocate for spaces that support healing and connection and serve vulnerable populations. Erin is also co-author of the "Designing for Peace Through a Trauma-Informed Perspective" chapter in the recently released *Peace by Design*, which provides a valuable overview of TiD concepts; and

* Graham Vickers, a director of justice architecture practice, focusing on secure environments that support rehabilitation, education, and health and wellness.

Their review was a tremendous effort, as we were rushing to get the book to print, and their participation provided checks from other viewpoints, protecting against unintentional harm and refining the text for precision and clarity.

We also thank Mary Haring, who's brilliant voice and promotional materials always make us look good. We are also grateful to Chana Haouzi, the founder of Architecture for Public Benefit, who designed and provided the renderings of the Trust and Transparency, Peer Support, and Choice domains. Thanks to her gracious offer to help, these visuals provide wonderful application examples for TiD practitioners.

Last, but very far from least, we thank Corin Hirsch for the book design and infographics contained herein. Corin was amazing to work with and turned our manuscript into a book we feel proud to present as a scholarly guide for those working in the field of Trauma-informed Design.

Thank you all for helping make this book a reality!

CONTENT ADVISORY

THIS BOOK CONTAINS INFORMATION RELATED TO THE FULL SCOPE OF trauma and the possible impacts it can have on those that have experienced traumatic events. It also includes discussions of current events and system-based inequities, in addition to survivor stories, case studies, and cautionary tales which are taken from real life. Engaging with this content may be emotionally challenging, upsetting, dysregulating, or triggering. All the material in this book has been carefully curated to provide practitioners with a background understanding of trauma, it's impacts, and trauma-informed care, as well as guidance on how to anticipate and mitigate stressors and potential triggers in the built environment and design spaces in which survivors can build resilience and heal.

If you find the content upsetting or dysregulating, please take the necessary steps for your emotional safety. You can step away from the content and engage in some grounding techniques, such as breathing exercises, drinking something and noticing how it feels as you swallow, taking a few moments to notice and name things in your surroundings, or thinking about your favorite things.

If you are struggling, please reach out to someone for support. You can talk to someone you know, or contact the:

* Substance Abuse and Mental Health Services Administration's National Helpline, at 1 (800) 622-4357 (HELP); or

* National Suicide Prevention Lifeline, at 1 (800) 273-8255.

INTRODUCTION

O UR PHYSICAL ENVIRONMENT CAN IMPACT OUR EMOTIONS AND behaviors, both negatively and positively. It has the ability to increase or reduce our stress levels. The spaces in which we live and receive services can communicate safety and promote supportive relationships, or they can symbolize lack of dignity and agency, which is further exacerbated for individuals who have experienced trauma.

The goal of Trauma-informed Design (TiD) is to create physical spaces that promote safety, resilience, and healing. This requires realizing how the physical environment affects identity, one's sense of worth, and dignity, and how it promotes empowerment.

We are frequently asked how TiD differs from typical adherence to "good design" principles. TiD is not an introduction of new design principles or features. It is a style of design practice, in which the primary goal is achieving a sense of safety for all users of the built environment and all participants of the design process. A sense of safety in the built environment is achieved by trying to understand the experiences of the people who will be occupying the space, and using that information to anticipate and mitigate stressors and potential triggers. This mitigation is often accomplished by techniques and features known to be "good design," which is why TiD environments may feel familiar to architects and designers.

A designer cannot achieve a TiD environment by simply applying "good design" principles, however. For example, there are times when a certain principle of "good design" may be stress-inducing or even triggering for the specific population of users. In such situations, the TiD practitioner is charged with thinking of alternatives that will achieve the same desired outcome while not jeopardizing the users' sense of safety in the environment.

TiD re-envisions the role of the designer and how the design process is conducted, with a goal of eliminating or minimizing all stressors and potential harms identified throughout the process, whether or not they are directly related to design. This means that TiD practitioners actively advocate for change when they identify client policies or practices that do not align with the principles of trauma-informed care or design and work to ensure all participants feel safe and supported throughout the design process. These are fundamental features of TiD; if overlooked or not done well, practitioners can cause harm to those involved.

The TiD Framework is a system for applying trauma-informed care, as originally established by the Substance Abuse and Mental Health Services Administration (SAMHSA), and continually evolving, into design. Trauma-informed care is based on an understanding of the prevalence and possible negative effects of trauma, and supports individuals through a system of universal precautions, actively resists their re-traumatization, and helps them build resilience.

In order to truly create a space that will support healing in survivors, it is important to cultivate an understanding of the people who will use the space, their identities and culture, and what is important to them, as well as the surrounding community. That understanding can then be used to anticipate and mitigate stressors and potential triggers, maximize choice, and create a safe, comfortable environment. As the users of the space develop a sense of safety, they can build resilience, strengthen their ability to emotionally regulate, and better access new opportunities.

This book is intended to serve as a manual and resource for TiD practitioners as they engage in this work. It lays out the ideal vision for a TiD design process, which we recognize is not always obtainable, given the parameters of specific projects, including budgets, building codes, the position of invested parties, and other constraints. TiD practitioners should strive towards fidelity with this model and carefully document their process and any barriers encountered along the way.

The book is divided into four main sections. The first chapters provide the background information necessary to understand the full scope and impacts of trauma. This is followed by an overview of trauma-informed care concepts. The remaining two sections address the practice of TiD more directly, first introducing the three spheres of this work, followed by the 11 domains and the TiD Framework itself.

The TiD Framework is built based on the most current scientific evidence available, which will continue evolving in the coming years. As such, we intend to update this work as new information alters the included understandings and approach. Although the Framework was developed by the TiD Society, based on SAMHSA's approach and design research, there are architects and designers already engaged in this work who share our understanding and will see many of their practices reflected.

We would like to address how a few terms are used throughout this book: client and survivor. As the TiD Framework is rooted in multiple disciplines, the word "client(s)" is used to refer to different (groups of) individual(s) in different parts of the book. Readers should use the context of the sentence to ascertain who the client(s) are. For example, in the context of a SAMHSA principle, "clients" are generally individuals receiving services. Similarly, when referring to organizations, "clients" are the people who buy or received products or services from the organization. When referring to architecture or design firms, however, "client" typically refers to the individual(s) or entity that engaged the services of the firm.

It is also valuable to address our use of the term "survivor." We use "survivor" to mean a person who has lived through a traumatic experience. We gave the use of this term significant consideration, as we recognize that some individuals who have had traumatic experiences do not self-identify as survivors. This may be because the term frequently implies that the person has risen above and beyond the experience, which is done and over, and relegated to the past. We know however, that, by definition, traumatic experiences infringe on a person's present and future. Still, we opted to use the word "survivor," because we see it as a term of empowerment. Anyone who has had a traumatic experience and continues on deserves to see themselves, and be seen by others, as triumphant, even if they are still dealing with the impacts on a regular basis. Despite this, we recognize that individuals who have experienced trauma may prefer different terms, and therefore recommend asking individuals about their preferred term and then using that term.

To help readers conceptualize some of the concepts addressed in this work, we have included survivor stories, case studies, and cautionary tales. While the stories are taken from real life, they have been de-identified. All names used in these examples have been changed to protect the anonymity of the individuals involved.

The practice of TID is hard. Presumably, practitioners enter this line of work because they want to make a positive difference in the lives of others. In doing so, they open themselves up to the stories of people who have experienced all sorts of hurt, violence, and harm. It is necessary to do this work well—but it also takes a toll.

We advise anyone entering this field to cultivate and nurture their resilience. In this book, we introduce a picture of what that could mean. We outline why caring for oneself as a TiD practitioner should go beyond what is typically referred to as "self-care." In order to do this work successfully and thrive, practitioners must gird themselves with supports, both external and internal, that will shield them when their stress levels inevitably rise. And so, we urge TiD practitioners to not leave their resilience-building as an afterthought, but to proactively build a multi-layered armor against the exposure that they will face.

There may come a time when even those closest to a TiD practitioner, members of their most devoted and loyal circle, may not understand their reactions to this work. In those times, it is helpful to have a community of other trauma-informed care and design practitioners who share and understand that experience. We therefore encourage those reading this book to reach out to us and others in this field to share resources, provide support, and build community.

1

UNDERSTANDING TRAUMA

I N ORDER TO UNDERSTAND THE CONCEPT OF TRAUMA-INFORMED DESIGN, it is essential to first understand the full scope of trauma.

According to the Substance Abuse and Mental Health Services Administration, "Individual trauma results from an event, series of events, or set of circumstances experienced by an individual as physically or emotionally harmful or life-threatening with lasting adverse effects on the individual's functioning and mental, physical, social, emotional, or spiritual well-being" (SAMHSA, 2014). This means that any experience can be considered traumatic if the individual believes it is physically or emotionally harmful or life-threatening and it has lasting negative effects on the individual throughout time (generally more than six months).

Trauma can come in many forms and presentations, well beyond what is commonly referred to as posttraumatic stress disorder (PTSD), which is usually tied to a specific incident or series of related events. In the following sections, we will explore the various types of trauma that a person can experience.

ADVERSE CHILDHOOD EXPERIENCES (ACES)

The immense impact early adversity can have on one's life was exposed due to a landmark study, published by Felitti et al. in 1998. Kaiser Permanente, a medical practice in California, noticed that some of their patients, who were participating in an obesity clinic, were doing significantly better than others with seemingly similar backgrounds. They wanted to identify why this was happening, and through discussions with the participants, they recognized that many of the patients who were struggling had experienced similar difficult things in their childhoods.

They identified 10 common things that these patients experienced prior to turning the age of 18, including: physical, emotional, and sexual abuse; physical and emotional neglect; and certain household stressors, including having a family member who was incarcerated, living with someone who had mental illness or a substance use disorder, witnessing domestic violence, or experiencing a divorce that led to a parent or caregiver being absent (Felitti et al., 1998). They called these experiences "Adverse Childhood Experiences" (ACEs).

The study mainstreamed the realization of a connection between early adversity and later poor health outcomes and risky behaviors. Up to that point, this was only recognized in the mental health field. The study also showed how common adversity is across all economic groups.

Prevalence and Impact of ACEs

Countless studies have shown that adverse childhood experiences can have lasting negative impacts throughout a person's life, including injury, impacts on mental health or maternal health, infections and chronic disease, the adoption of risky behaviors, and the loss of opportunities.

ACEs were shown to have a dose response: across virtually all categories, the more ACEs a person experiences, the more they are at risk for negative outcomes. The original study found this direct correlation for each of the following health risks:

Alcoholism and alcohol abuse

Ischemic heart disease

Sexually transmitted diseases

Risk for sexual violence

Chronic obstructive pulmonary disease

Health-related quality of life

Risk for intimate partner violence

Unintended pregnancies

Early initiation of smoking

Poor academic achievement

Early initiation of sexual activity

Suicide attempt

Fetal death

Financial stress

Depression

Illicit drug use

Liver disease

Poor work performance

Smoking

Multiple sexual partners

Adolescent pregnancy

(Felitti et al., 1998)

The data also showed that people with high ACE scores are more likely to have more broken bones, necessary medications, auto-immune diseases, and work absences. People with four or more ACEs were:

* 390% more likely to have chronic obstructive pulmonary disease(COPD), such as emphysema or chronic bronchitis;
* At a 240% greater risk of hepatitis or sexually transmitted disease;
* 32 times more likely to have learning and behavior problems;
* At 10-12 times greater risk of attempted suicide and drug usage later in life;
* Seven times more likely to be an alcoholic;
* 4.5 times more likely to experience depression; and
* Three times more likely to experience asthma, cancer, and heart disease (Felitti et al., 1998).

People with six or more ACEs died nearly 20 years earlier, on average, than those without any ACEs (Felitti et al., 1998).

Since the original study, the term "adverse childhood experiences" has been expanded to include any experience in a person's childhood that has similar negative health impacts. All states now collect ACE data through a random telephone survey called the Behavioral Risk Factor Surveillance System (BRFSS). The BRFSS measures the prevalence of ACEs, but as it is conducted through telephone surveys, its data is believed to be an underrepresentation of the true level of traumatic exposure across the nation. The BRFSS data from 2001 to 2020 indicates that 64 percent of the adult population in the United States have experienced at least one adverse childhood experience (Swedo et al., 2023).

Disproportional Impact of ACEs on Marginalized Communities

People with disabilities are more at risk to experience ACEs than the general population (Centers for Disease Control and Prevention, 2021). The frequency of ACEs is also more likely to be higher in children with special health needs. Children with ACEs are more likely to: have a chronic medical condition; have ongoing emotional, developmental, or behavioral concerns; or either, experience being bullied, or engage in bullying behavior. They are less likely to: have mothers who are reported to be in "very good" or "excellent" physical and mental health; engage in school; or live in families that feel hopeful during difficult times (The Child and Adolescent Health Measurement Initiative, 2019).

There are racial disparities as well. Reports of ACEs vary significantly by race or ethnicity and household income. At 36.2%, American Indian/Alaska Native families reported the highest percentage of children with two or more ACEs, while the lowest was reported by Asian families (6.0%). Across race/ethnicity groups, the percentage of children with two or more ACEs decrease as household income increases (Health Resources and Services Administration Maternal and Child Health Bureau Maternal and Child Health Bureau, 2020). The results also show that Black children are:

* Reported to have a higher number of ACEs than white children; and
* Over-represented among children with two or more ACEs (Lanier, 2020).

TRAUMA BEYOND ACES

The idea of ACEs does not encompass all forms of potentially traumatic events that a person may experience, because difficult experiences can happen at any point in a person's life, not only during childhood. As such, ACEs are only a small portion of what could be considered traumatic, and ACE data should not be used to estimate a population's exposure to trauma (Anda et al, 2020).

It is not possible to catalog every potentially traumatic event, in part because life events are so varied and numerous, and because what may be traumatic for one person may not be for someone else. This is a key point going forward: whether an experience is traumatic is dependent on how the person it happens to experiences it.

> **Whether an experience is traumatic is dependent on how the person it happens to experiences it.**

SAMHSA's definition of trauma includes three components:

1. The specific experience that happens to the individual;
2. The individual **has to believe** it is physically or emotionally harmful or life-threatening; and
3. It has to have lasting negative effects on the individual throughout time.

Using this individual-centered definition of trauma, we can see how the list of things that might be traumatic could be infinite.

Trauma can take on different forms:

* There are **acute traumas.** These are usually one-time events such as an accident, death of a loved one, weather event, or assault.
* Trauma can also be **chronic,** or occurring over time, such as ongoing abuse or neglect, combat situations, or even multiple unrelated traumas.

* Trauma can be incredibly **complex,** such as repeated uprooting, homelessness, human trafficking, living as a refugee, or experiencing more than one type of ongoing abuse/neglect.
* There are **system-induced traumas,** such as the removal of a child from a family and placement in foster care, sibling separation, having to testify in court against family, and living in extreme poverty.

Social Determinants of Health

There is a strong relationship between trauma and the **social determinants of health** (SDOH). Just like trauma, the SDOH are nonmedical factors that influence health outcomes. According to the United States Center for Disease Control and Prevention (CDC), SDOH "are the conditions in the environments where people are born, live, learn, work, play, worship, and age that affect a wide range of health, functioning, and quality-of-life outcomes and risks," and can be sorted into five domains: economic stability; education access and quality; health care access and quality; neighborhood and built environment; and social and community context (CDC, 2024).

In an effort to more accurately describe SDOH, some recommend using the term "social influences of health," because there is not a direct causal relationship to health outcomes. Nonetheless, SDOH can positively or negatively impact a person's health, well-being, and quality of life.

Examples of SDOH include safe neighborhoods, racism, violence, quality education, job opportunities, clean outdoor spaces, polluted water, accessibility of nutritious foods, access to health services, and language and literacy skills. This list illustrates that many of the poor outcomes from SDOH stem from systemic inequities often found in areas with lower socioeconomic status and marginalized communities (World Health Organization, n.d.; CDC, 2024).

The science is clear: when a person lives in an adverse community environment or experiences inequities, it can have the same negative impact on their long-term health outcomes as other traumas. We see the same dose response as for other traumas. The

> **The science is clear: when a person lives in an adverse community environment or experiences inequities, it can have the same negative impact on their long-term health outcomes as other traumas.**

impact of these inequities can be compounded over generations, or when a person is a member of more than one marginalized group. In short, experiencing inequity can be traumatic.

In 2015, the World Mental Health Survey Consortium indicated that over 70 percent of people experience at least one traumatic event in their lifetime, with 30.5 percent of them experiencing four or more (Benjet et al., 2016). In the United States, 2013 data showed 90 percent of adults reported exposure to at least one traumatic event, with women reporting higher rates than men, including in the categories of direct interpersonal violence, sexual assault, and physical assault (Kilpatrick et al., 2013). It stands to reason that these rates may even be higher following the recent COVID-19 global pandemic.

The Three Realms of Trauma

Trauma can result from more than just personal events. We can conceptualize traumatic events as occurring in three realms: household or personal; community; and environmental.

Household and Personal Trauma

Many household or personal traumas stem from adverse childhood experiences, or from **intergenerational trauma.** Intergenerational trauma occurs when a parent passes the effects of their own trauma onto their children, often because their trauma keeps them from sufficiently meeting their children's needs. This often begins in the child's infancy, during the early attachment phase.

Attachment

In a healthy caregiver-infant relationship, a child learns about their impact in the world through something called the attachment cycle.

The cycle begins with the child comfortable and at rest. The child then experiences discomfort or a need. They express their need, usually by the only means available to them, by crying. Hearing the child cry, the attentive caregiver responds, usually picks the child up, and makes eye contact. Typically, they talk or otherwise try to soothe the child. This calms the child, and the child begins to trust that when they cry out, their caregiver will come to their rescue. As the child's peace is restored, they engage, often playfully, with their caregiver, and return to a state of rest—until they experience another discomfort and the cycle begins again.

The frequent repetition of this "secure attachment cycle" is pivotal in forming some of the child's fundamental understandings of the world and how it works. Their experience is that, when they express a need, someone responds to help

Secure Attachment Cycle

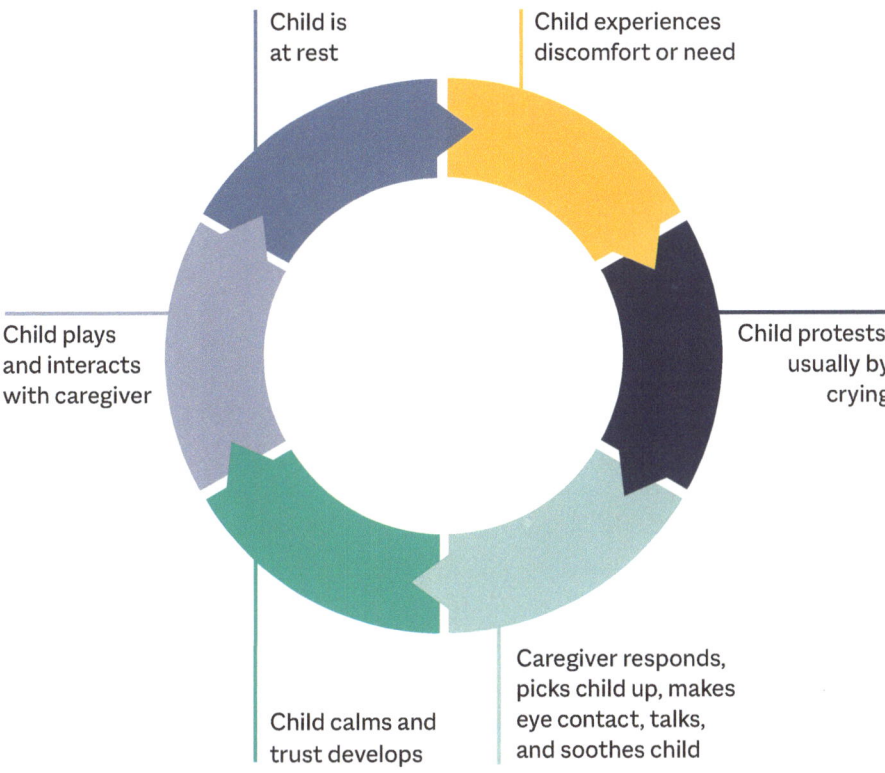

Figure 1. Secure attachment cycle

them. This leads them to develop the belief that connection to others can lead to their needs being met. They start to see others as fundamentally good and worthy of trust, and see themselves as worthy of love and acceptance. They feel safe, and subconsciously form the belief that the world is a safe place.

In situations of early abuse or neglect, however, the attachment cycle can be disrupted. This happens when the caregiver's response is frequently absent or inconsistent.

The cycle begins the same, with the child at rest, who then experiences discomfort and cries out. In this scenario, however, the caregiver does not respond to the child, or responds inconsistently. Not able to help themselves, the child does the only thing it can in hopes of getting its need met—it cries louder. Unfortunately, this does not bring about the desired result. The caregiver either responds with anger or resentment, or does not respond at all. The child gives up. They do not

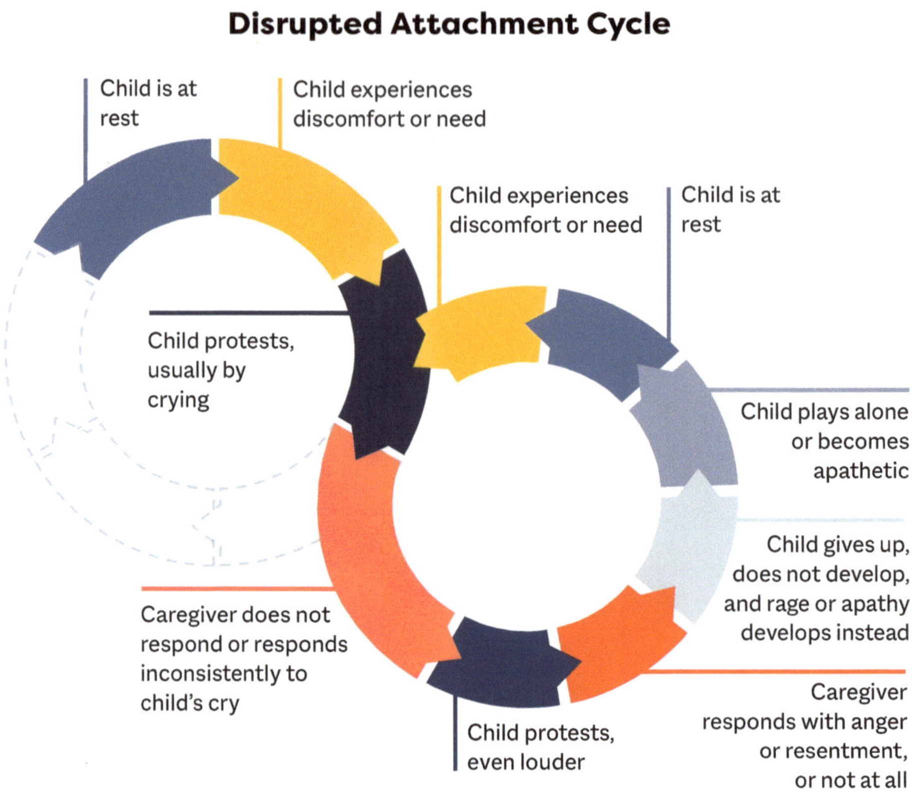

Disrupted Attachment Cycle

Child is at rest

Child experiences discomfort or need

Child experiences discomfort or need

Child is at rest

Child protests, usually by crying

Child plays alone or becomes apathetic

Child gives up, does not develop, and rage or apathy develops instead

Caregiver does not respond or responds inconsistently to child's cry

Caregiver responds with anger or resentment, or not at all

Child protests, even louder

Figure 2. Disrupted attachment cycle

develop trust. Instead, they begin to develop apathy or rage. With no hope of help, the child either entertains themselves or loses interest in engaging with the world around them. Eventually, the cycle continues, reinforcing these negative outcomes.

Children who experience this "disrupted attachment cycle" develop a very different view of the world. They begin to feel angry and ashamed and believe they have to find a way to meet their own needs however they can. As a result they believe the world is a dangerous place and that they cannot trust anyone. They do not develop the sense that they are worthy of love and care.

Because the needs of children in this situation are not consistently met, they do not develop an understanding of how their actions impact others. This can lead to difficulty understanding the cause-and-effect relationship, which further impacts their ability to form healthy social relationships. They may become overly independent, to the point that they engage in cycles of self-sabotage that confirm their core belief that things will never go well for them. As they age, they may engage in behavior that violates rules and laws, because they often rebel against external forces trying to control their behavior, and they have difficulty comprehending systems built on rewards and consequences.

While ACEs and intergenerational trauma account for a large portion of this realm, household or personal traumas are not restricted to things that occur during childhood. A person can experience abuse, violence, or an acute traumatic experience at any age. Living with, or caring for someone with, a chronic illness can also be experienced as a household or personal trauma, as can being involved in an extended legal battle.

Community Trauma

Community traumas are caused by the societal systems under which we live, and are sometimes referred to as "adverse community environments" (Ellis and Dietz, 2017). This type of trauma is produced by structural violence, which prevents people and communities from meeting their basic needs, such as war, terrorist attacks, civil unrest, racism, poverty, and poor housing. The result of an adverse

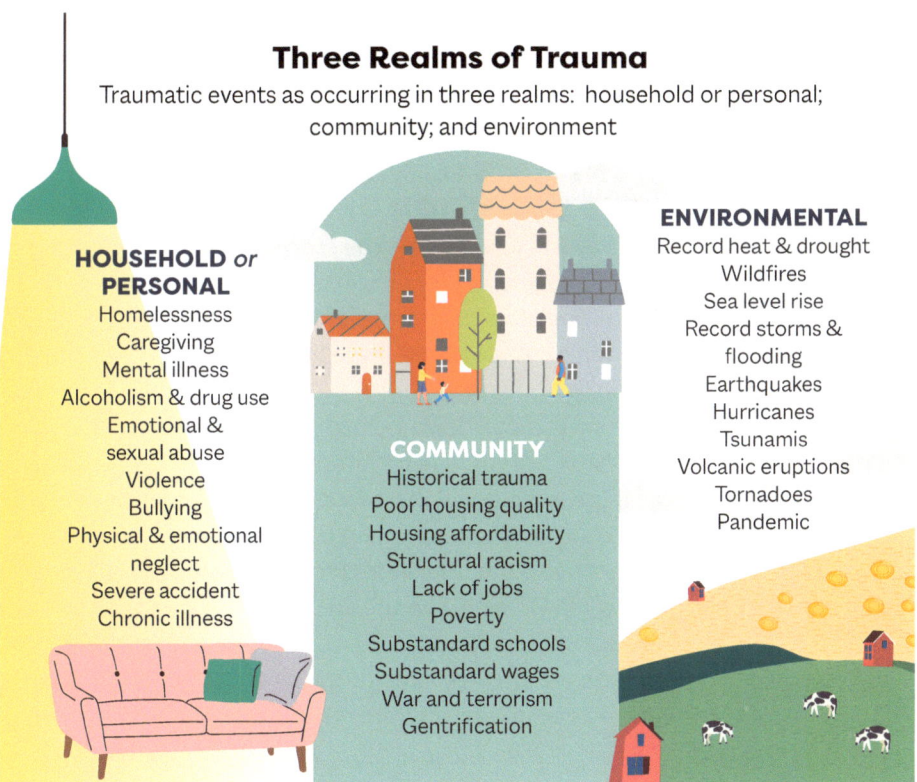

Three Realms of Trauma

Traumatic events as occurring in three realms: household or personal; community; and environment

HOUSEHOLD or PERSONAL
Homelessness
Caregiving
Mental illness
Alcoholism & drug use
Emotional & sexual abuse
Violence
Bullying
Physical & emotional neglect
Severe accident
Chronic illness

COMMUNITY
Historical trauma
Poor housing quality
Housing affordability
Structural racism
Lack of jobs
Poverty
Substandard schools
Substandard wages
War and terrorism
Gentrification

ENVIRONMENTAL
Record heat & drought
Wildfires
Sea level rise
Record storms & flooding
Earthquakes
Hurricanes
Tsunamis
Volcanic eruptions
Tornadoes
Pandemic

Figure 3. Three realms of trauma

community environment is both: high levels of trauma across the population and a breakdown of social networks, relationships, and positive social norms across the community.

Trauma can also extend beyond the individuals who directly witness or experience violent events. Take a community affected by a school shooting, for example. If a significant portion of the people in the community are affected, the very way the community interacts can change. This change then impacts community members who were not directly involved.

Environmental Trauma

We now recognize that natural disasters and climate crises can also be traumatic. Droughts restrict access to food and other necessary resources. Some environmental events, such as hurricanes, wildfires, pandemics, volcanic eruptions, and tsunamis, can displace entire regions. Others, such as tornadoes and earthquakes, tend to have a sporadic, but equally devastating, effect on communities.

Traumatic events stemming from each of the three realms (household or personal; community; or environment) intertwine throughout people's lives, and affect the viability of families, communities, organizations, and systems.

CURRENT EVENTS, SYSTEM-BASED INEQUITIES, AND THE EVOLUTION OF TRAUMA

As the human experience is ever-evolving, so is the scope of trauma. Environmental traumas can be localized, regional, or global. Similarly, community traumas can be based on regional inequities or have international reach. Civil unrest, terror attacks, and war are community traumas that have a deep and pervasive impact on the communities involved.

Collective trauma is a term used to describe a significant negative event that shatters the basic fabric of a society. It affects entire groups of people, communities, or societies. It can impact relationships, change policies and governmental processes, alter the way the society functions, and even change social norms.

Examples of recent collective traumas include the September 11, 2001 attacks on the United States, the war in Ukraine, and the October 7, 2023 attack in Israel and the ensuing Israel-Hamas war.

Below is a more detailed look at three specific types of community traumas: gentrification; the COVID-19 pandemic; and the social justice movement in the US of 2020 – 2022.

Gentrification

Gentrification is the process through which the character of a highly populated urban residential area often associated with poverty is changed by wealthier people moving in, improving housing, and attracting new businesses. This type of neighborhood change displaces the existing inhabitants and often results from "urban renewal" efforts or "revitalization" plans. The consequences of these types of projects can be significantly damaging.

According to the CDC, gentrification is a housing, economic, and health issue that affects a community's history and culture and reduces social capital. Displacement of residents has health implications that contribute to disparities among vulnerable communities, including lower-income and elderly residents, women, children, and members of racial or ethnic marginalized groups (CDC, 2013).

These populations are at increased risk for the negative consequences of gentrification. Studies indicate that vulnerable populations typically have shorter life expectancy; higher cancer rates; more birth defects; greater infant mortality; and higher incidence of asthma, diabetes, and cardiovascular disease. In addition, increasing evidence shows that these populations have an unequal share of residential exposure to hazardous substances such as lead paint (CDC, 2013).

Other effects that impact displaced residents include limited access to, or availability of:

* Affordable healthy housing;
* Healthy food choices;
* Transportation choices;
* Quality schools;
* Bicycle and walking paths;
* Exercise facilities; and
* Social networks (CDC, 2013).

TiD practitioners recognize that these displaced communities experience a type of systemically-created inequity that could be experienced as traumatic. Changes can occur in stress levels, rates of injuries, the level of violence and crime, mental health, and social and environmental justice. It is important that development be well-thought-out and culturally appropriate for the neighborhood and existing residents, lest we contribute to the long-term harmful effects of gentrification.

COVID-19 Pandemic

Many people have reported experiencing the COVID-19 pandemic or its effects as traumatic. During the height of the pandemic, almost everyone in the world experienced isolation on some level. Social gatherings were restricted, and how much time we could spend in-person with others was limited. The impacts on mental health were significant, as social isolation can lead to increased depression and suicidal ideation.

Most people also experienced at least some loss of autonomy. New rules forced changes in our routines and processes. Many workers were laid off or had to quickly pivot to remote work for the first time. Other "essential employees" were required to report to work despite the risks. It is worth noting that these employees were overwhelmingly from marginalized communities who already faced higher risk for poor outcomes if they contracted the virus.

People experienced loss on multiple levels. In addition to deaths and illness, many experienced the ambiguous loss that comes from changing or absent social norms, rituals, and rites of passage. Often people struggling with ambiguous loss find it difficult to discuss these losses or seek comfort from others. This can stem from feeling as though their loss is not significant or "real" enough, compared to what others have been through.

In addition to these almost universal impacts, a segment of the population coped with a heightened fear of contracting the virus because they or someone close to them was at higher risk for poor outcomes. There were also some people living in unsafe homes who were confined to those homes and faced increased danger. The restrictions in movement also increased food insecurity, especially for children who were receiving free or reduced lunches at school.

Healthcare workers also experienced a magnified impact, especially at the beginning of the pandemic. Not only did they treat those with severe respiratory distress, they were sometimes called on to decide which patients would be put on extracorporeal membrane oxygenation (ECMO) machines when there were not enough machines for the number of patients who needed them. They sat with dying patients when families were not allowed to visit and, at the end of the day, could not even return home to their own families or support systems. The emotional toll lead to many leaving the profession.

Any of these impacts could have been experienced as traumatic, and they were all magnified for those who had already experienced previous trauma.

Social Justice Movement of 2020–2022

While the world was battling COVID-19, the United States was experiencing a social justice movement unlike any in decades. Spurred by the public and video recorded murders of Ahmaud Arbery and George Floyd, many Americans became aware of the disproportionately high number of Black people killed by police in the US for the first time. This resulted in many calling for an end to policies and practices they saw as the crux of systematic racism.

Rallies, protests, marches, and camp-outs flooded the nation, sometimes turning violent. There were calls to defund, and even abolish, the police. Over time, there were clashes between protesters and police, sometimes ending tragically. As the movement unfolded, many BIPOC individuals and law enforcement officials experienced it as traumatic, regardless of whether they were directly involved.

These events demonstrated the divisions in the population, erosion of trust in our government, and the difference in how Black, Indigenous, and People of Color (BIPOC) are treated by law enforcement was highlighted. Since then, the social justice campaigns have waned, but the American public is now more aware of the inequities that exist in our society. As a result, inequitable situations are more likely to raise attention and flood the airwaves, exposing Americans to traumatic stories and visuals on a more regular basis.

TOXIC STRESS

To understand what makes something traumatic, we have to talk about stress. We all experience stress in our lives, which we can think of as being on a continuum.

If a person does the same thing repeatedly, with no changes, they are in their **comfort zone.**

To learn something new, the person has to step outside their comfort zone, at least a little. This causes the person to experience stress. When the person is feeling relatively safe, this stress does not result in any lasting negative impacts, and the person can learn from the experience. This is referred to as **positive stress.**

Toxic stress is the mechanism by which adversity becomes traumatic.

When the person experiences higher levels of stress, they can become quite uncomfortable. They may feel nervous or anxious, or experience biological responses, such as a racing heart, sweating, or constricted vision. When the experience is relatively short, or the person has someone with whom they can process it with afterwards, the person typically realizes that they were unharmed and remained safe. With this perspective, they might consider trying again, and even come to enjoy similar experiences in the future. This is referred to as **tolerable stress.**

If the person's boundaries get pushed even further, so that they honestly feel as though their life is in danger and there is no end in sight, and they have no one to process the situation with afterward, their stress levels can rise to a level referred to as toxic stress.

Toxic stress is the mechanism by which adversity becomes traumatic.

Two people may experience the same thing, and it may be traumatic to one, but not the other. Genetics has something to do with this, as both anxiety and depression are genetically heritable. Very frequently, however, the difference is whether the person has a supportive adult to rely on.

A child can live through a high number of adverse experiences yet develop into a healthy adult and do extremely well in life. These outcomes are often experienced by those who had a relationship with at least one reliable adult who was a constant in their life, and showed them that they were worthy of love and valuable as a human being, just as they were. This is because the adult buffered the child from what would otherwise be toxic levels of stress. Even without directly addressing the child's negative experiences, the relationship created an environment in which the child's stress could subside and their system could rest.

This explains why some might experience an event as traumatic, but not others. If the adversity is not buffered or counterbalanced with supportive relationships and the types of experiences and emotions that lower stress, it can become toxic. Anything that creates toxic stress can be traumatic. Examples not yet mentioned include living with chronic health issues, caring for an adult relative for an extended period of time, and prolonged legal or emotional battles.

IMPACTS OF TRAUMA

I T IS NECESSARY TO UNDERSTAND THE EFFECTS AND SYMPTOMS OF TOXIC stress and trauma so that TiD practitioners can design effective solutions to mitigate their impact.

EFFECTS OF TRAUMA ON THE BRAIN

Figure 4 below is a model of the human brain useful in understanding the impact of trauma.

The outer, blue-gray portion of the image represents the prefrontal cortex (PFC), sometimes referred to as the "thinking center" or "logic brain." This is the part of the brain with which we form coherent, logical thought. The prefrontal cortex is the seat of the brain's ability to: regulate attention and awareness; make decisions about the best response to a situation; initiate conscious, voluntary behavior; determine the meaning and emotional significance of events; regulate emotions; and inhibit or correct dysfunctional reactions.

The green portion in the high-center of the brain illustration represents the "emotional center" of the brain. This is part of the limbic system, and the part of the brain that forms relationships and attachments.

The yellow stem protruding out the bottom represents what is sometimes referred to as the "reptilian" or "survival brain," which is linked to your amygdala. Evolutionarily, this is the oldest part of the brain. It is the part of the brain that: detects threats in the environment and activates stress responses; activates the sympathetic nervous system (SNS) to help the person deal with the threat (for more information regarding stress responses and the SNS, see the section on the polyvagal theory); and helps store new emotional or threat-related memories.

Trauma & Brain Development

When a person is concerned about their survival, they have fewer resources to devote to social-emotional and more complex logical thought

| Typical development | vs. | Developmental trauma |

Typically, humans do not think much about what they need to do to stay alive, such as breathe and control their body, so they can focus on social-emotional and logical thought. When a person has experienced significant trauma, however, they need to focus more of their energy on basic survival tasks, so they have fewer resources to devote to social-emotional and more complex logical thought.

When a person's brain detects a threat, the amygdala, or survival brain, releases adrenaline, norepinephrine to accelerate their brain and body. This evolutionary response is optimized for survival, happens before the individual can evaluate what is occurring, and can therefore not be voluntarily controlled. Adrenaline's main function is to quickly prepare the body to flee or fight its way out of a dangerous situation. Norepinephrine is both a neurotransmitter and a hormone that increases alertness, constricts the blood vessels to maintain blood pressure, and activates the initial stress response (Cleveland Clinic, 2024a and 2024c).

Should the threat continue, the amygdala communicates with the hypothalamus and pituitary gland to release cortisol, which is sometimes called the "stress hormone." Cortisol typically helps suppress inflammation and regulate key body systems, including its metabolism, blood pressure, blood sugar, and sleep-wake cycle. During times of high stress, cortisol is released to keep the body on high alert and trigger the release of glucose to fuel the body through its response (Cleveland Clinic, 2024b).

While all this is happening, the medial part of the prefrontal cortex, which is slower, assesses how significant the threat really is. Based on that assessment, it can then either accentuate or calm down the stress response.

Following trauma, brain scans show a hyper-reactive amygdala and a less-activated medial prefrontal cortex (van der Kolk, 2015). Their amygdalae release an excess of norepinephrine, which results in hyperarousal, hypervigilance, increased wakefulness, and sleep disruption. Their prefrontal cortexes are impaired in their ability to regulate the threat response, which can result in less control over reactive anger and impulsive behaviors when they are emotionally activated.

Effects on Instinct and Mood

The limbic system is a system of nerves and networks in the brain, involving several areas concerned with instinct and mood. It controls basic emotions, such as fear, pleasure, and anger; and drives, including hunger, sex, dominance, and care of offspring.

As described above, cortisol is released when a person experiences stress. This causes an increase in heart rate and blood pressure. Levels of cortisol can become too high in a person experiencing toxic stress, resulting in: increased blood sugar levels; weight gain; a suppressed immune system; digestive problems; and heart disease.

It is worth noting that the weight gain evidenced from high cortisol is due to false hunger signals, not because the person is overeating to find comfort in their sad, emotional state. Their body is signaling that they are hungry and need food. It generates cravings for high-fat, high-calorie foods that will prepare the individual for the impending fight or escape necessary to ensure their survival.

Effects on Memory

Trauma can affect a person's memory in various ways, including impacts on semantic, episodic, emotional, and procedural memory.

Semantic memory is a person's ability to remember basic facts, including vocabulary. The impact on semantic memory is why a person may not be able to recall words, or may find it difficult to do math calculations that they once considered easy, following an accident or traumatic event. Some trauma survivors have suggested they feel as though they are no longer as smart as they were prior to the event.

Episodic memory relates to a person's ability to recall incidents, as they occurred, in the order they occurred. When trauma affects a person's episodic memory, they may not be able to recount a story reliably. The details or the sequence of events may change. This disordered thinking is why victims of violent crimes can sometimes be viewed as unreliable witnesses.

When a person is suddenly overcome with emotions related to a trauma, often seemingly with no cause, it is referred to as an emotional memory. An example of this is when a person who has been injured in a war zone hears a loud noise and suddenly experiences fear, a racing heart, and extreme alertness. They may even brace themselves for impact or duck for cover.

Procedural memory is a person's ability to do something routine without actively thinking about it. A person's procedural memory can be affected by trauma, which is why, for example, a person who has experienced a stroke or traumatic brain injury may have to relearn how to walk or talk.

EPIGENETICS AND EXPOSURE TO TOXIC STRESS

Epigenetics is the study of biological mechanisms that change the expression of a person's genes. A person's genes have "markers" that can either express themselves or not. Research indicates that exposure to toxic stress or traumatic events may result in changes to genetic markers, causing some to "flip" and express themselves when they previously did not, or vice versa.

While the fertilization process can wipe some genetic markers from DNA, there is increasing evidence that these flipped markers can then be passed down through generations. According to one study, male descendants of Confederate prisoners-of-war seemed to suffer transgenerational trauma (Costa et al, 2018), as evidenced by their mortality rate and health. Sons of the prisoners who were born after the war had an 11 percent higher mortality rate, mostly due to cerebral hemorrhage. They were also more likely to be obese and die from cancer. The prisoner's grandsons also had a higher mortality rate than the general population. These effects were not present in the female descendants of the prisoners, nor in children born prior to the war.

In 2014, a study of the women who survived the Tutsi genocide in Rwanda and their children found that the women and their children had identical alterations of their genes. Among other things, these changes were associated with lower cortisol levels (Perroud et al., 2014). In 2015, a similar study found children of Holocaust survivors had epigenetic changes to a gene that was linked to their levels of cortisol (Yehuda et al., 2015).

A more recent study indicated that adult offspring of women survivors of the Tutsi genocide experienced secondary traumatization and are more prone to depression, anxiety, and panic attacks (Bonumwezi et al., 2024).

While it is difficult to isolate if changes in human behaviors are the result of genetic changes or similar parenting patterns adopted by survivors of a shared traumatic experience, a study in mice allowed for the offspring to be removed immediately after birth. This study involved emitting an electrical current across the bottom of the mice's cage every time a certain scent was released. The mice learned to avoid standing directly on the cage whenever they smelled that particular scent. The removed offspring were then raised in a different environment that was never electrified. Still, the offspring tried to avoid the bottom of the cage whenever the scent was released into their environment. After a few generations of mice who never experienced the pain along with the scent, the reaction was "unlearned" by descendants (Dias and Ressler, 2014).

SYMPTOMS OF TRAUMA

The symptoms of trauma can be categorized as being cognitive, behavioral, physical, and psychological. These symptoms can be grouped into three categories:

* Symptoms that can lead to behaviors that might be misinterpreted as a person refusing to cooperate;
* Symptoms appear from the hypervigilance, or constant state of arousal, that can result from trauma. These things can make observers feel as though the person is being intentionally hostile, especially when they are feeling threatened; and
* Symptoms that are often overlooked, because the person may show no outward signs of distress.

Hyperarousal and Hypoarousal

Typically, people operate with a range of emotions. They can get excited, or be calm, or anywhere in between. This normal range is referred to as a person's "window of tolerance" (Siegel, 1999).

When a person experiences a traumatic event, their reactions can include bigger swings, and be somewhat heightened or deflated, extending beyond their normal range. When this happens, we refer to the person as being **"dysregulated."**

A person can even get stuck outside their window of tolerance. This is when they can experience hyperarousal or hypoarousal.

Hyperarousal is caused by an overactive fight or flight stress response (for more information regarding stress responses, see the section on the polyvagal theory). The person may experience any of the symptoms that can appear as refusal to cooperate, including: confusion and disorientation; nausea; digestive problems; loss of memory and concentration; nightmares or insomnia; aches and pains throughout the body; tremendous fatigue and exhaustion; anxiety, fear, trembling, or panic attacks; emotional flooding and intrusive thoughts of the event, sometimes occurring out of the blue. Other symptoms of hyperarousal may appear more

Window of Tolerance

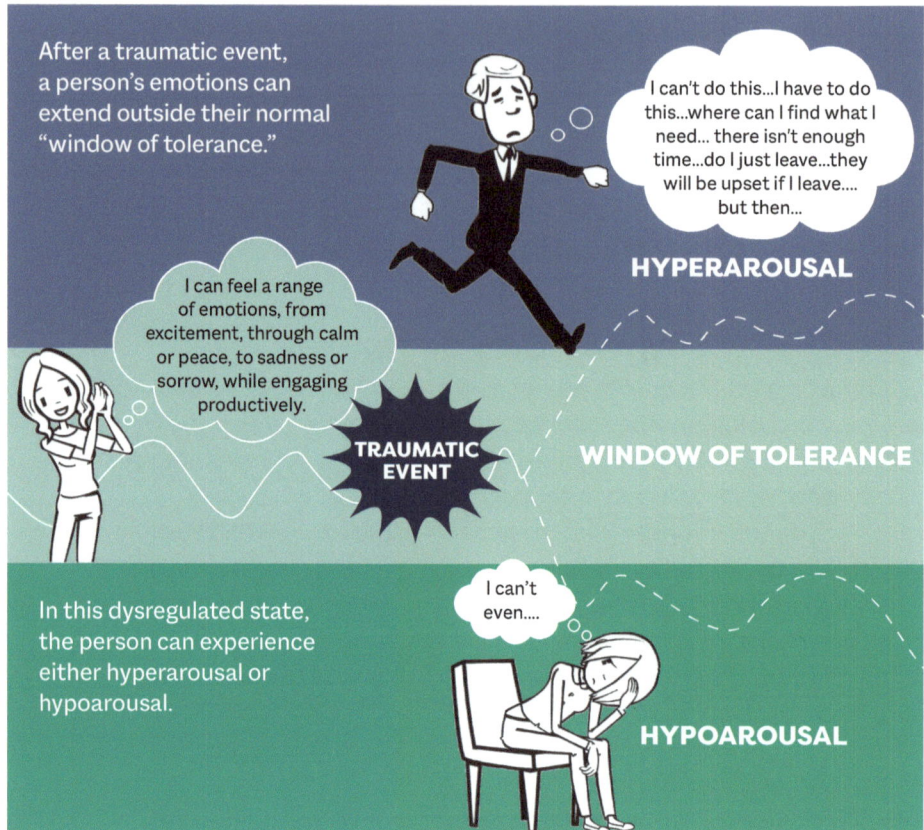

Figure 5. Window of tolerance

like the person is being intentionally hostile, including hyperactivity; outbursts of anger or rage; being easily startled; avoiding direct eye contact; a racing heartbeat; an inability to relax; restlessness; sleeplessness; extreme alertness against danger; mood swings, edginess, and agitation; and chronic muscle patterns or tension. The chronic muscle patterns or tension can lead to sudden, jerky movements. If a person is always tense, their muscles can react in spasms, leading them to accidentally strike someone nearby.

On the opposite end, **hypoarousal** is caused by an overactive freeze response. This results in the symptoms that are often overlooked. The person may display a flat affect or experience: confusion and disorientation; nausea; loss of memory and concentration; depression; anxiety, fear, trembling, or panic attacks; lethargy; nightmares or insomnia; tremendous fatigue and exhaustion; chronic fatigue; discon-

Survivor Story 1: Hyperarousal

John had a history of getting into trouble. Growing up, he was always in the principal's office for mouthing off and disrespectful behavior. This morning, he lost his job. It wasn't fair. He completed his work, but wasn't willing to pick up others' slack just because they messed around all day. At the end of his shift, when his boss ordered him to stay late until all the work was done, he yelled back that he wasn't a slave and walked out.

What Was Really Happening

John was worried that if he stayed late, he'd miss his bus. He had to get to the office in time to pay his electric bill or his power would be shut off. He promised his girlfriend he wouldn't let that happen again, and he had done everything right. Why should he pay the price because someone else was goofing off?

Even though John had worked hard to learn new ways to communicate when he was upset, was so stressed thinking of the potential fall-out that he couldn't think clearly in the moment, explain himself, or respond to his boss' request in a respectful manner. In his state of hyperarousal, he lashed out.

nection; dissociation; aches and pains throughout the body; low blood pressure; poor digestion; or intrusive thoughts of the event, sometimes occurring out of the blue. People experiencing hypoarousal are frequently labeled as lazy, unreliable, unwilling to try, or having their head in the clouds.

Stress Responses

When a person reacts to a threat from their survival brain, without assessing level of danger logically, it is referred to as a **stress response.** Stress responses are activated as a survival mechanism in response to threats. They are very rapid responses that do not allow time for logical thought processes.

The fight or flight responses of hyperarousal and the freeze reaction of hypoarousal are all stress responses. The reaction is almost instantaneous. The brain sends a signal to the body and the reaction happens before the person can recognize what is happening. Therefore, when a stress response is activated, the individual cannot choose to respond differently until their prefrontal cortex has had time to catch up, which may take time.

Imagine a person in a dark, cobwebbed basement. They feel something on their shoulder, startle, and immediately jerk their head to look, raise their hand towards

Survivor Story 2: Hypoarousal

Jessica attended the same suburban middle school as her two older brothers. She had always done well previously, but the transition to the larger school was difficult for her. In just a few months she had wracked up several incompletes and was failing most of her courses. She frequently failed quizzes and tests, despite studying and knowing the material at home.

Recognizing that the level of autonomy granted to students in middle school to manage their workloads was significantly >> greater than in younger grades, Jessica's teachers assumed she needed additional support to develop the necessary executive functioning skills. They created a system of check-ins and parent communication to develop accountability, but Jessica still struggled. Upon further inquiry, it became clear that she frequently completed her homework, but failed to turn it in. Either she left it at home, or it accumulated at the bottom of her locker or backpack.

Jessica's parents and teachers became frustrated with what they saw as a lack of caring and self-sabotage. She was clearly smart enough to understand the material, and often completed not only the homework, but even extra credit assignments, in an attempt to raise her grade. Why then, did she just not care enough to hand them in? If she was trying to hurt someone, it was only hurting herself.

What Was Really Happening
Jessica was overwhelmed with her new school and the level at which she was expected to perform. Her brothers had always been honors students, and she knew she couldn't live up to the expectations of her teachers or parents. In addition to school, she was involved in both sports and the drama club, all of which seemed like crushing responsibilities.

When she was able to regulate and focus, Jessica could complete homework and other assignments. The minute she stepped into school, however, her stress levels started to rise, and she couldn't remember any of it. Jessica's teachers and parents did not recognize that she was actually in a state of hypoarousal at school.

their shoulder, and somewhat jump to the side. A moment later, they realize what they felt was their hair and not a spider or hand reaching out to grab them. This example demonstrates how the reaction can be completely absent logical thought, even when the threat is fairly benign.

In addition to the three identified stress responses (i.e., fight, flight, freeze), there are other responses to threats that can serve to avoid or minimize harm. One that has received significant attention recently is the "fawn" or "please and appease" response. This is when the individual tries to pacify, please, and cater to the needs of the person presenting the threat, even to the point of neglecting their own personal needs and boundaries. Unlike a stress response, however, the fawn response is based in logical thought.

The fawn response is a learned, adaptive behavior to mitigate harm. The person using this approach has learned being agreeable can make things easier, and so they use it to placate the source of danger. Overtime, repeated use of the fawn response can become unconscious, especially if it is adopted at a young age. However, it is not automatic, and with time, the person can learn strategies to center themselves and fawn less as their skills grow.

The distinction between the stress responses of fight, flight and freeze and other trauma responses that can minimize harm, such as fawn, is important to keep in mind when thinking about trauma-informed care and design because it delineates a point at which the person can choose, or use, a behavior—even if that choice is subconscious—versus when they experience an uncontrollable reaction.

TRAUMA TRIGGERS

A trauma trigger is a stimulus that sets off a memory of a trauma or a specific portion of a traumatic experience. Sensory reminders of the traumatic event, such as noises, smells, temperatures, physical sensations, or visual scenes, are often triggers. Triggers may be caused by interactions with others and are frequently associated with the time of day, or a season, holiday, or anniversary of the event.

When a person experiences a trigger, they believe, and respond as though, the past traumatic event is happening in the present. The individual truly believes their life or well-being is in imminent danger, and they have to do whatever is necessary to survive. While the person is experiencing the trigger, they are limited in their ability to control their behavior and logically consider its consequences.

Common triggers include: unpredictability; sensory overload; feeling vulnerable or frustrated; confrontation; and experiencing something that reminds the person, even at a subconscious level, of a past traumatic event.

Survivor Story 3: Triggered

Mark spent his early years living on the streets. He frequently did not have access to clean water or enough to eat, and sometimes went days without a meal.

At the age of seven, Mark was adopted by a family that always had an abundance of food. As he previously never new when, or if, he'd eat again, Mark ate as much as he could at every meal. It took several months before he was able to moderate his food intake and only eat when he was hungry. Overtime, Mark developed a healthy relationship with food.

When he was 14 years old, his family went on a rural vacation abroad. They stayed in apartments and planned to prepare breakfasts and dinners themselves, and eat lunch out. Unfortunately, they had difficulty accessing markets while they were open and found there weren't many restaurants. Sometimes the family went several hours between meals, with only granola bars and other snacks to tide them over.

When they did find food, Mark gorged himself and ate until he felt sick. One evening towards the end of the trip, he asked to order a second meal. Recognizing his distress, his parents let him. When it was served, he packed it up in its entirety for lunch the next day.

What Was Really Happening

When Mark experienced hunger, it triggered his survival response. He started eating uncontrollably when there was food, and was no longer able to moderate his intake. He did not return to healthy eating patterns until several days after returning home, where the refrigerator, freezer, and pantry were stocked with food he could access at any time.

STRESS DISORDERS

Individuals who experience intense symptoms following a traumatic event, including flashbacks, nightmares, severe anxiety, uncontrollable thoughts about the event, and reminder avoidance, may be diagnosed with **post-traumatic stress disorder** (PTSD). PTSD is typically related to a specific incident or a series of related events, and the flashbacks associated with PTSD are often experienced as a sensory re-living of the causal event(s).

When a person experiences prolonged trauma, they can develop a condition known as **complex post-traumatic stress disorder** (CPTSD). CPTSD presents much like PTSD, but may also experience difficulty with emotional regulation, sense of self, and relationships. The flashbacks experienced by a person with CPTSD are also different from PTSD flashbacks. Most CPTSD flashbacks are emotion-based, in which the individual experiences sudden, intense emotions such as fear, shame, alienation, rage, grief, or depression, without a direct memory or understanding of what caused the reaction (Walker, n.d.; WellMind Counseling, 2024). While CPTSD is not included as a distinct condition in the Diagnostic and Statistical Manual of Mental Disorders (DSM-5), it is broadly recognized among mental health professionals worldwide and was included in the international Classification of Diseases (ICD) in 2019.

TRAUMA-INFORMED CARE

T HE TRAUMA-INFORMED DESIGN FRAMEWORK IS A SYSTEM FOR applying trauma-informed care to design. Trauma-informed care is based on an understanding of the prevalence and possible negative effects of trauma, and enacts a system of universal precautions to support individuals, resist their re-traumatization, and help them build resilience. What follows is a brief overview of several key concepts of trauma-informed care.

UNIVERSAL PRECAUTIONS IN RESPONSE TO TRAUMA

Short of witnessing it or a person disclosing their experience, there is no way to know if a person has experienced trauma. People are often able to mask its signs. Given the widespread prevalence of trauma, we recommend adopting a "universal precaution" approach. This means assuming anyone might have gone through a traumatic experience at some point and adjusting our interactions with everyone, so that we do not accidentally retraumatize someone who has.

A STRENGTHS-BASED APPROACH TO RESILIENCE

When seeing a person who is unable to regulate their emotions or experiencing a stress response, a person who is not trauma-informed may wonder "what's wrong" with them. This can lead them to develop judgements and wrong conclusions.

Similarly, there is a school of thought that urges professionals to consider "what happened to" someone who seems dysregulated. Often, however, that is a significant overstep of the person's privacy and can wrongly focus professionals on "fixing" the individual. Even if it is relevant to the work we are engaging in, asking too many intensely personal details can disrupt the relationship and erode trust. It is important to remember that it is not necessary to know what caused a trauma response to be able to effectively help.

We recommend a third option: considering "what's right with" the individual, and helping them build on their strengths. This holistic approach identifies a person's positive attributes and empowers individuals to engage in resilience-building.

Resilience is the ability to overcome serious hardship. Building a person's resilience is the primary way to protect against the risks associated with trauma. By forming strong relationships and sharing positive experiences, we can buffer a person's stress, help them build resilience, and interrupt the negative effects of trauma. This lays the groundwork for a shift to positive outcomes and experiences.

Research shows that the positive experiences we have with others can counteract the possible negative impacts of traumatic experiences. In fact, positive social experiences are so powerful, a person can have fewer positive experiences than negative ones, yet still experience increased resilience (Bethell et al., 2019).

SAMHSA'S CONCEPT OF A TRAUMA-INFORMED APPROACH

SAMHSA's concept of a trauma-informed approach is grounded in four assumptions and six principles (SAMHSA, 2014).

SAMHSA's Four Assumptions ("The Four Rs")
According to SAMHSA:

> A program, organization, or system that is trauma-informed realizes the widespread impact of trauma and understands potential paths for recovery; recognizes the signs and symptoms of trauma in clients, families, staff, and others involved with the system; and responds by fully integrating knowledge about trauma into policies, procedures, and practices, and seeks to actively resist re-traumatization (SAMHSA, 2014).

The previous pages of this framework have outlined information to aid in the realization of the impact of trauma and recognition of its signs and symptoms. Moving forward, the framework will outline potential paths for recovery.

To provide Trauma-informed Design services, practitioners have to respond by fully integrating this knowledge into their policies, procedures, and practices;

recommendations provided to their client; and ultimately, their designs, to actively resist re-traumatization.

SAMHSA's Six Key Principles

SAMHSA has also identified six key principles of a trauma-informed approach (SAMHSA, 2014). Each of these principles is built into the TiD Framework. They are:

* Safety;
* Trustworthiness and Transparency;
* Peer Support;
* Collaboration and Mutuality;
* Empowerment, Voice, and Choice; and
* Cultural, Historical, and Gender Awareness.

Understanding how SAMHSA conceptualizes its six key principles enables TiD practitioners to apply them to design. What follows is an overview of these principles.

Safety

Safety is the highest priority in implementing a trauma-informed approach. The SAMHSA principle states:

> Throughout the organization, staff and the people they serve, whether children or adults, feel physically and psychologically safe; the physical setting is safe and interpersonal interactions promote a sense of safety. Understanding safety as defined by those served is a high priority (SAMHSA, 2014).

Safety is about both: physical and psychological safety. It's not only about the physical setting. Ensure individuals feel safe with the interpersonal interactions taking place is integral to a trauma-informed approach.

It is equally important to recognize that this is about how the situation feels to each individual involved in a situation. This means it is not enough that the professionals, or those with power in the relationship, believe the situation is safe. If any of the involved people do not feel safe, this key principle has not been achieved.

The principle of safety applies to everyone, everywhere, and every interaction—including staff, clients, and children. It is

Safety is the highest priority in implementing a trauma-informed approach.

Survivor Story 4: Feeling Unsafe

Maria was a very athletic veteran, who was learning to ski. As a hard-charging, multiple-sport-playing, never-give-up, and fairly-skilled client, she mastered the learning area's two trails before lunch. It was a beautiful day, and she and her instructor decided to take a longer beginner's run that traversed its way down most the mountain after their break. She did great, until she arrived at the final, somewhat steeper pitch. By this time, her legs were tired, and when she saw the drop to the lodge, she froze.

This initial surge of fear was a common reaction when first-timers saw the steeper terrain. Maria sat down, however, and despite her conviction that she would ski down, no amount of coaxing, rationalization, or attempts at slowly making their way down would get her to budge.

Maria was, objectively, safe. She and her instructor were off to the side of the hill, out of the way of other skiers. They could walk to the lodge in a few minutes if they wanted, or even take a ski patrol sled or snow mobile down. Nonetheless, it took over an hour for her instructor to successfully convince her to try and coach her down the final descent.

What Was Really Happening

Maria didn't *feel* safe, despite knowing that there was little risk to her physical safety. Due to her tendency to push through challenges, she'd have felt like a failure if she did not ski down. Also in her mind, if she tried to ski down, she would fall on her already injured shoulder and do irreparable damage, keeping her from the sport she loved best. Maria was an avid volleyball player, and her community of friends were all involved in her sport. She was worried that falling on the snow would result in her losing both her favorite pastime and all her closest connections. And so, she was frozen in place.

paramount because we know that when a person is not feeling safe, their stress levels can get too high, leading to difficulty regulating, and possibly a stress response or trigger. They may even experience the interaction as traumatic. We cannot be trauma-informed while creating further harm.

To create a safe environment, we cultivate trustworthiness, set and enforce clear and consistent boundaries, interact with transparency and predictability, and offer choice. Asking the person if there is anything you can do to help them feel more safe gives them power and a voice in safeguarding their wellbeing. In addition to asking this question of clients directly and regularly, a trauma-informed approach encourages clients and others to ask for support whenever necessary, and to name specific things they believe will help when they feel unsafe.

Trustworthiness and Transparency

SAMHSA explains the principle of trustworthiness and transparency in the following way:

> Organizational operations and decisions are conducted with transparency with the goal of building and maintaining trust with clients and family members, among staff, and others involved in the organization (SAMHSA, 2014).

Operating in a transparent fashion is crucial to developing a trusting relationship with clients, family members, staff, and others involved in the organization. Trust is vital to developing strong relationships and fostering a sense of safety. It is through strong relationships that we can buffer others' stress levels, and help them build resilience and heal from traumatic events.

When working to develop trust, it is important to remember that some individuals with traumatic pasts may have experienced or witnessed relationships being used as a threat. This may have included: violence in a relationship; the types of grooming or abusive behaviors that are common in toxic relationships; a family member, partner, or loved one threatening to leave the relationship unless the person does what they demand; or real abandonment or neglect. When a person experiences these types of relationship dynamics, they often internalize the situation and believe they, themselves, are at fault for causing the situation. It can be very difficult to build trust with someone with this type of history, and the relationship may need to be developed slowly over time.

Showing respect and compassion, working together towards a common goal, and letting others see our commitment to the relationship over time, even if difficult situations arise, are all ways to develop trust.

Peer Support

The SAMHSA principle of peer support is about people with similar lived experiences of trauma mutually supporting one another through the healing journey:

> Peer support and mutual self-help are key vehicles for establishing safety and hope, building trust, enhancing collaboration, and utilizing their stories and lived experience to promote recovery and healing. The term

"Peers" refers to individuals with lived experiences of trauma, or in the case of children this may be family members of children who have experienced traumatic events and are key caregivers in their recovery. Peers have also been referred to as "trauma survivors" (SAMHSA, 2014).

The inclusion of peer support in SAMHSA's approach indicates a recognition that those with similar experiences can more deeply understand and relate to a person's experience, and that being included in a peer group can help a survivor not feel so alone or different. It provides the individual with a group of people with whom they can talk freely and process the event at a time when they may feel misunderstood or distanced from their family and friends.

Collaboration and Mutuality

The SAMHSA principle of collaboration and mutuality is about forging relationships between staff and clients and throughout the organization, regardless of power structures:

> Importance is placed on partnering and leveling the power differences between staff and clients and among organizational staff from clerical and housekeeping personnel, to professional staff and administrators, demonstrating that healing happens in relationships and the meaningful sharing of power and decision-making. The organization recognizes that everyone has a role to play in a trauma-informed approach. As one expert stated: "one does not have to be a therapist to be therapeutic" (SAMHSA, 2014).

According to this principle, everyone has a role in delivering a trauma-informed approach. You never know who will be able to forge the relationships that help a person build resilience. This is about opening the door and building relationships that transcend structure and work together towards a common goal.

When working collaboratively with individuals or communities, it is important to remember that each of us sees the world through the lens of our own experiences, which forms our understanding. As a result, multiple people can experience the same event, and each be impacted differently. It is important to recognize that each response is valid and look for a way forward that benefits everyone involved.

Empowerment, Voice, and Choice

Under the SAMHSA model, staff are facilitators, and clients are empowered to use their strengths to support their recovery. The principle of empowerment, voice, and choice states:

Throughout the organization and among the clients served, individuals' strengths and experiences are recognized and built upon. The organization fosters a belief in the primacy of the people being served, in resilience, and the ability of individuals, organizations, and communities to heal and promote recovery from trauma. The organization understands that the experience of trauma may be a unifying aspect in the lives of those who run the organization, who provide the services, and/or who come to the organization for assistance and support. As such, operations, workforce development and services are organized to foster empowerment for staff and clients alike. Organizations understand the importance of power differentials and ways in which clients, historically, have been diminished in voice and choice and are often recipients of coercive treatment. Clients are supported in shared decision-making, choice, and goal setting to determine the plan of action they need to heal and move forward. They are supported in cultivating self-advocacy skills. Staff are facilitators of recovery rather than controllers of recovery. Staff are empowered to do their work as well as possible by adequate organizational support. This is a parallel process as staff need to feel safe, as much as people receiving services. (SAMHSA, 2014).

This principle recognizes that people who have experienced traumatic events often feel as though they have lost power over their own lives. It raises our consciousness to the fact that, historically, many have had their control over their own bodies and health choices diminished and have been the recipients of forced or coercive treatment. This practice continues in modern day, as individuals may face criminal charges or imprisonment, or risk losing their children, if they are not successful in meeting substance use treatment requirements set by courts or diversion programs, for example. During the COVID-19 pandemic, many essential workers were required to get vaccinated or face losing their jobs, even if they had a legitimate medical reason contraindication. The principle of empowerment, voice, and choice works to stand against these types of coercive treatments and instead involve patients in determining their own paths to wellness.

The goal of collaboration and mutuality is that clients advocate for themselves. Often, however, people from marginalized groups or with significant trauma histories have not had the opportunity to practice much choice in their lives, or to develop the skill of self-advocacy. We can support them while they develop this skill by learning their perspective and advocating for them until they are able to do so for themselves. This can serve as a living example of what that advocacy looks like, while we coach them in using positive and effective approaches.

Often, this support begins with helping the individual become more comfortable with making choices. An individual who has always been limited in choice, for example, may find too many options overwhelming. When working with this individual, we can control the amount of choice, or the risks associated with choosing, to build their confidence. They can start with small, relatively inconsequential choices, and tackle more significant situations as they become more comfortable. If they make a choice with undesirable consequences, we can support them through the experience, so they can build up their tolerance and learn to see mistakes as learning opportunities rather than insurmountable obstacles.

The Staff Experience
The principle of empowerment, voice, and choice also calls our attention to the staff experience. Not only may staff have their own experiences of trauma, they are exposed to the traumatic experiences of clients on a regular basis. This can lead to vicarious trauma, which results from being exposed to other's firsthand traumatic experiences.

Individuals in professions that expose them to high rates of others' traumatic experiences should regularly engage in self-care, to protect against the development of vicarious trauma. This can include anything that regulates their nervous system, including exercise, practicing mindfulness or grounding activities, spending time with family or friends, engaging in hobbies, practicing a faith, spending time with members of their chosen community (e.g., faith, club), or even creating lists and checking them each off as they are completed.

Self-care is only part of the picture, however, and in a trauma-informed system, staff should be provided with robust "co-care" by others in the organization and community. This is essential, because when stress is high, it is hardest to practice self-care. This co-care can occur on multiple levels:

* **Families can:** share concerns and help develop supportive strategies; try not to take stress-fueled reactions personally; maintain daily life

> **It raises our consciousness to the fact that, historically, many have had their control over their own bodies and health choices diminished and have been the recipients of forced or coercive treatment.**

routines; discuss the demands of the job and its impacts on family members; engage in social, creative, and self-care activities; and seek mental health services.

* **Coworkers can:** reach out and discuss the impact of the work; help establish consistent work-to-home transitions that create a boundary and safe place outside the workplace; encourage sleep, healthy eating, hygiene, and exercise; support connections with family, friends, and coworkers; and refer someone who is struggling to peer support or employee assistance programs, and encourage them to discuss the situation with their supervisor.

* **Supervisors can:** discuss vicarious trauma as part of supervision; encourage time off, and allow flexible work schedules when possible, while staying attuned to the possibility of withdrawal or isolation; demonstrate self-care by engaging in it themselves and including resiliency-building activities into meetings and other everyday practices; allow time on the job for staff to engage in peer support, assistance programs, and mental health services; and refer staff who are struggling to assistance program and mental health services.

* **Organizations can:** provide mechanisms that allow staff to take meaningful breaks to regulate as needed; encourage staff to take time off; build systems that allow staff to completely disconnect when doing so, without returning to unmanageable workloads; offer staff education and professional development opportunities to build resiliency skills; provide fitness center memberships free or at a reduced cost; provide efficient and ready access to wellness programs, assistance programs, and mental health services.

The exposure risk of developing vicarious trauma applies to TiD practitioners as well. To combat this, we need to be supported by our organization through co-care, personally engage in self-care, and encourage our coworkers and clients to do the same. We need to demonstrate that we value ourselves as we value others.

Cultural, Historical, and Gender Awareness
SAMSHA's principle of cultural historical and gender awareness roughly equates to having an equity lens:

The organization actively moves past cultural stereotypes and biases (e.g., based on race, ethnicity, sexual orientation, age, religion, gender-identity, geography, etc.); offers, access to gender responsive services; leverages the healing value of traditional cultural connections; incorporates policies, protocols, and processes that are responsive to the racial, ethnic and cultural needs of individuals served; and recognizes and addresses historical trauma (SAMHSA, 2014).

This is a strong directive for organizations seeking to adopt a trauma-informed approach. In other words: you can't be trauma-informed un unless you are actively working to identify and dismantle inequities.

SAMHSA's stance is based on the evidence that experiencing inequities can have the same health impacts as other traumas. As such, a trauma-informed approach builds relationships that shatter stereotypes and support the empowerment of all people, regardless of to which groups they belong, or are perceived to belong. It must acknowledge that racism is systematically built into our lives on every level, and be responsive to the racial, ethnic, and cultural needs of clients. Similarly, it must be gender-responsive, with the recognition that, throughout history, our society has been structured in a way that has granted certain privileges to cisgender men. These are non-negotiable elements of a trauma-informed approach, as they are vital to ensuring the safety of clients and staff and helping us create healing relationships and environments.

> **You can't be trauma-informed unless you are actively working to identify and dismantle inequities.**

SAMHSA's Recommended Implementation

In recognition that a trauma-informed approach requires change and systematic alignment throughout multiple levels of an organization, SAMHSA also identified areas in which the six key principles should be applied for successful implementation. They are:

* Governance and Leadership;
* Policy;
* Physical Environment;
* Engagement and Involvement;
* Cross-sector Collaboration;
* Screening, Assessment, and Treatment Services;

* Training and Workforce Development;
* Progress Monitoring and Quality Assurance;
* Financing; and
* Evaluation (SAMHSA, 2014).

For an organization to be fully trauma-informed, it is necessary that all aspects of its structure, operations, management, and practices are reviewed with a trauma-informed lens to ensure that they are actively resisting re-traumatization. For TiD practitioners, this will most come into play when evaluating and adjusting their own organization and developing TiD recommendations for clients.

More information on implementing an organization-wide trauma-informed approach can be found int SAMHSA's Practical Guide for Implementing a Trauma-Informed Approach (SAMHSA, 2023).

COMMUNITY CARE

Just as an individual can lean on family or friend during stressful times, communities can be a source of support and aid in reliance-building. Healthy communities provide an infrastructure of services that can help individuals and families better meet their needs. In such communities, parents who are struggling, for example, can not only be supported by neighbors, they can turn to community organizations and services, such a parenting classes, drop-in day care providers, or behavioral health centers. This is a form of co-care, in which the community provides care through readily available and accessible services that meet the individual's needs.

In some situations, the culture of an organization can become significantly affected by one or more individual who is dysregulated. When this happens, community care can provide supports and services intended to help staff and clients return to a more regulated state. When the organization is part of a larger system, the system can transfer in experienced staff members from outside the affected program, to support the staff and clients who have been impacted. An organization that provides transitional housing in a number of distinct locations, for example, can relocate staff to an affected program to ensure a fresh, stabilizing presence in the home. Based on the circumstances, the organization may even wish to move some of the residents to different locations so that other, more resilient residents can enter the home. This type of careful community management can serve to restore the program to a more desirable state.

POLYVAGAL THEORY

The polyvagal theory is a model for understanding the states of the autonomic nervous system (ANS), which can impact our behavior, especially when stressed. The ANS regulates a person's heart rate, blood pressure, breathing, digestion, and other involuntary actions that support life (Harvard Health Publishing Staff, 2024). It responds to signals of danger and threat to initiate life-preservation activities.

The polyvagal theory provides an understanding of a person's sense of safety and the states that define their window of tolerance. According to the theory, when a person feels safe, it promotes spontaneous social engagement behaviors. In this state, the person's heart rate slows and digestion initiates, their eyes soften and are able to connect with others, their hearing is enhanced, and their facial muscles are more reactive. The theory goes on to explain that a person's autonomic state is optimized during safe social interactions, which recruit neural circuits that support health, growth, and restoration (Porges, 2020).

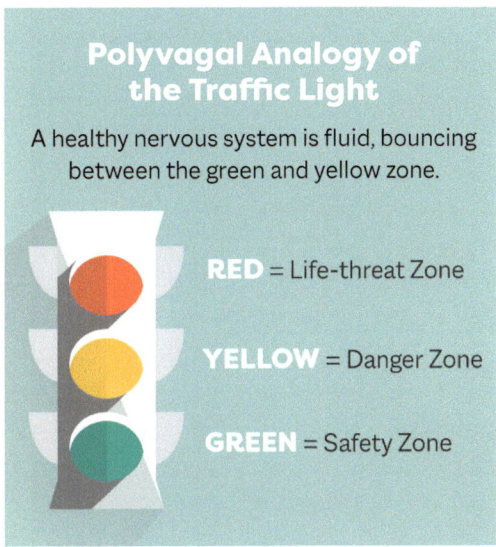

Figure 6. Polyvagal traffic light

Similarly, when a person is receiving cues of danger or life-threat and is feeling unsafe, they go into a state of defense, firing neural circuits that disrupt bodily processes. When a person senses danger, their heart rate increases, sensations of pain increase, and their muscles prepare to either flee or fight off the threat. In this state, the person's facial control and hearing may be limited. If the danger is so extreme that it could be life-threatening, the individual's muscle tone is compromised and they freeze or shut down. Porges uses a stop light to explain these states, with green being the safety zone, yellow the danger zone, and red the life-threat zone (Porges, 2020).

The polyvagal theory identified that social behavior is embedded in the neural regulation of mammals. Because our systems are optimized when we are feeling safe and engaging socially, our bodies remain healthier when we can co-regulate with others, especially through play (Porges, 2020).

Crucial to understanding the polyvagal theory is knowing that unlike other, more primitive lifeforms, mammals have two branches of the vagus nerve, called the ventral vagus and the dorsal vagus. The ventral vagus is myelinated, or enclosed in a sheath of fatty substance that makes it more efficient and rapid. The dorsal vagus nerve is more primitive and unmyelinated. In addition, almost all animals have a sympathetic nervous system (SNS), which developed very early in evolutionary history. The SNS controls the animal's fight or flight response.

The ventral vagus nerve is located in the brain stem, and is connected to our ability to make eye contact and control our facial expressions and tone of voice— all necessary to maintain social understandings and relationships. Following trauma, survivors often have difficulties with these abilities, as well as with emotional regulation, listening, and following directions. They may experience speech or language delays, sound sensitivities, or difficulty swallowing—all of which are tied to the ventral vagus nerve (Porges, 2020).

Nervous System Circuits

Together the circuits created by the two vagus nerves and SNS comprise our ANS. The three primary circuits that impact our ability to regulate our nervous systems are therefore called: the ventral vagal complex (VVC), the dorsal vagal complex (DVC), and the SNS. When we are feeling safe, our VVC circuit is operating, and we are able to engage in social interactions. When we begin to receive cues of danger, the SNS circuit kicks in, resulting in mobilization and activating either a fight or flight response. If the danger rises to a level that we perceive to be life-threatening, the DVC circuit shuts-off our ability to react, conserves all our energy by minimizing our body's metabolic demands, and immobilizes us. This can be in the form of fainting, shutting down, or dissociating (Porges, 2020).

Physiological States of the Nervous System

Our systems can engage the circuits within its nervous system alone or together, creating a total of six different states. When operating by themselves, each circuit results in its own physiological state.

The VVC fosters a state of social interaction and communication, In this state, we experience normal heart rate and muscle tone, and we may feel relaxed, engaged, curious, or hopeful (Polyvagal Institute, n.d.).

The engagement of the SNS leads to mobilization. In this state we experience increased heart rate, blood pressure, hormone flow and muscle tone. How we feel when our SNS is engaged depends on if we are feeling safe. If we are, we may feel energetic, active, playful or motivated. If, on the other hand, we sense a threat, we may feel stressed, anxious, or fearful, and the SNS activates a fight or flight response (Polyvagal Institute, n.d.).

The engagement of the DVC results in immobilization. In this state we experience a low heart rate, as well as low muscle tone and energy. Similar to the SNS, our sense of safety affects how we feel when the DVC is engaged. When we are feeling safe, we may feel blissful, dreamy, tranquil, or meditative. If we are feeling unsafe, we may feel depressed, unhappy, lonely, or hopeless. This can result in shut-down or dissociation (Polyvagal Institute, n.d.).

We experience additional physiological states when two circuits operate at the same time. By linking:

* The VVC with the SNS, we experience play, dance, sports, and performance, which are enjoyable forms of interaction and moving together;
* The SNS with the DVC, we experience freeze. In the polyvagal theory, freeze is considered a hybrid state of these two circuits, because it is not a complete shut-down state and we still have muscle tone; and
* The VVC with the DVC, we experience quiet moments and intimacy. In this state, we remain accessible while being immobilized (Porges, 2020).

Heart Rate Variability

Heart rate variability (HRV) is a measure of the variation in time between each heartbeat (Harvard Health Publishing Staff, 2024). Data shows that HRV tends to be lower in people in a mobilized state than in those experiencing relaxation

Physiological States of the Polyvagal Theory

We experience different physiological states based on which nervous system circuits are operating.

Dorsal Vagal Complex (DVC)
Sympathetic Nervous System (SNS)
Ventral Vagal Complex (VVC)

Shut down or disssociation •
Freeze ••
Quiet moments and intimacy ••
Fight or flight •
Play, dance, sports, and performance ••
Social communication •

Figure 7. Polyvagal physiological states

or immobilization. This suggests that people with a high HRV may have greater cardiovascular fitness and be more resilient to stress (Harvard Health Publishing Staff, 2024).

Studies show that we can reduce the reactivity of our ANS, and thereby increase our window of tolerance, by engaging in activities that alter our HRV, including yoga, body work, and movement. Even more beneficial are activities that involve movement while also integrating the social engagement system, such as making music with others, engaging in play, and petting an animal (Porges, 2020).

Since its introduction, parts of the polyvagal theory have come under criticism, as there is no traditional scientific evidence to support that that the ventral vagus is evolutionarily newer than the dorsal vagus or that it functions the way Porges claims. There is, however, significant qualitative data to support the theory's accuracy—not the least of which is grounded in the results experienced by survivors who engage in polyvagal-based therapies.

Quantitative methods have long been the standard for accepted scientific research. By carefully constructing studies, researchers can control for unknown variables and systematically draw, and build on, conclusions. In contrast, qualitative research has been dismissed as less rigorous and prone to bias. In recent years, however, researchers have begun to question that assumption and noted that quantitative research tends to maintain accepted beliefs, limits critiques, and provides support for misconceptions about marginalized groups. (Arellano, 2022; Santoro, 2023). With increasing awareness of the importance of cultural relevance, it has become more clear that the stories collected as part of qualitative research have immeasurable value in deciphering trends, especially when there are disparate impacts on marginalized communities (St George et al., 2023; Ford & Goger, 2021).

It is with this understanding in mind that we are obliged to consider the countless survivors who have reported benefiting from polyvagal-based therapies and exercises. Countless studies have indicated improved emotional regulation, a heightened sense of safety and self-empowerment, increased self-compassion, reduced anxiety, and greater connection with others. The volume of evidence supporting the effectiveness of these strategies cannot be ignored. In fact, the United States military has used vagal stimulation with veterans to improve their outcomes and is moving toward incorporating it in military training.

By understanding the polyvagal theory and what types of activities can impact the ANS, we can recognize when a person is dysregulated. We can also adopt, and encourage others to engage in, movement, breathwork, humming, and social activities that expand our window of tolerance and help us better regulate when stressed.

PLAY THEORY

There is a collection of scientific research that examines the purpose and benefits of play, commonly referred to as "play theory." Studies on play are generated from several fields, including: psychology, including educational and evolutionary psychology; neuroscience; and ethology, or the field observation of animal behavior. This research indicates that play is the foundation of learning, social and communication development, problem solving, strategic thinking, and relationship and skill development.

Animal studies show that play is linked with evolution. While all mammals, as well as birds and some reptiles, are born with the instinct to play, species with larger brains are more playful in their youth (National Institute for Play, 2024). Studies also suggest the more playful an animal is in youth, the longer life expectancy it may have (Fagen & Fagen, 2009, National Institute for Play, 2024).

In humans, play has been shown to be the foundation of learning, problem solving, and strategic thinking, as it allows us to explore our environments and acquire new concepts. Piaget's cognitive development theory outlines stages of development and how the play experiences help a child explore and make sense of the world around them. Through play, children actively engage in the environment and use their hands to explore. This allows them to experiment and adapt their understanding of the world by assimilating new experiences into existing knowledge or creating new schemas to accommodate novel situations (McLeod, 2024b).

Play is also linked to developing emotional intelligence and increased personal and social well-being. Erickson's theory of psychosocial development focuses on the social and emotional aspects of human development across the entire lifespan (McLeod, 2024a). The theory outlines eight stages of psychosocial development, from infancy to adulthood, that must be successfully completed in order to develop a healthy personality and sense of self. It posed that that opportunities for individual and group play that encourage exploration, problem-solving, and self expression throughout one's lifespan are important to explore emotions, build self esteem, and development of strong identities. It is also worth noting that Erickson's first stage, "trust versus mistrust," is based on the caregiver's consistency and responsiveness of care. As discussed in the Attachment section earlier in this book, early abuse or neglect during this stage can impact a child's sense of self and their ability to impact others and the world around them.

Frobel's play theory suggests that play is the natural and essential activity of young children and, through play, children can represent their thoughts, emotions, and experiences in symbolic and creative ways. He saw the importance of nature in play and learning (Merrick, 2022). Outdoor activities and environments can encourage connections to nature and build on children's curiosity of the environment and promote a sense of wonder. According to this theory, play should be a joyful experience. Environments should be positive and nurturing where children feel safe to explore, take risks, and make mistakes without fear of judgement (Maynard & Waters, 2014).

Maria Montessori and Reggio Emilia are two educators who viewed play as an essential part of learning. They both paid considerable attention to how a child's physical environment fostered play-based learning. Montessori's concept is a child-led play approach to learning, supported by age-appropriate activities and resources. It recognized the importance of experiential sensory experiences in the child's cognitive development. To that end, play-based environments should include opportunities for sensory exploration, such as natural materials and tactile, visual, and auditory activities (Jones, 2024).

The Emilia theory emphasizes the impact the physical environment, relationships, and creativity can have on an child's well-being. The physical environment is considered the third teacher, and spaces are designed to be aesthetically pleasing, inviting, and flexible, to promote a child's exploration and collaboration. The theory also encourages collaborative learning experiences and group-play opportunities to promote the development of cooperation, communication, negotiation, social skills, and empathy (Reggio Emilia Early Learning Centre, 2024).

These theories clearly demonstrate that play is a crucial part of a child's development that helps them build essential capabilities. By engaging in purposeful play, children develop social, emotional, and cognitive abilities, engage their imagination, take risks, and learn how to problem-solve. On the other hand, a deprivation of play can lead to depression and impulsive behavior, and interfere with social and emotional development and learning (National Institute for Play, 2024). This is in part because play helps us test and learn social boundaries, but also because early play with infants develops attunement between a child and its caregiver (National Institute for Play, 2024).

Attunement is a caregiver's ability to recognize and respond to their child's needs (Child Development Institute, 2020). It is necessary to develop a healthy attachment—a key building block for developing healthy relationships. As we know that strong, healthy relationships are a vital part of counteracting the impacts of trauma, and that a deprivation of play can impact our ability to form such relationships, we can see why play is an important aspect of a trauma-informed approach, for all ages.

Adults can engage in play in many ways, including art, music, board or video games, sports, or other athletic activities. As long as a person is engaging with others or their surroundings and enjoying the experience, theses activities can aide survivors in reclaiming their sense of safety, finding ways to express emotions, reconnecting with their bodies, and building resilience. Play gives the freedom to explore, create, and make meaningful connections with the world around us. Embracing playfulness delivers a path to self discovery, healing, and empowerment for survivors (Goodyear-Brown, 2019).

TRAUMA-INFORMED DESIGN

T RAUMA-INFORMED DESIGN IS ABOUT INTEGRATING THE PRINCIPLES of trauma-informed care into design, with the goal of creating physical spaces that promote safety, well-being and healing. This requires realizing how the physical environment affects identity, worth and dignity, and how it promotes empowerment.

Environments have the ability to increase or reduce our stress. By anticipating and mitigating potential triggers, TiD practitioners can create spaces in which users' stress systems can rest and they can find peace. In this peace, they can then form supportive relationships with adults who can challenge and support them through healing.

The two fundamental things to focus on when approaching trauma-informed design are to:

* Get to know who will be using the space and what is important to them; and
* Use that understanding to anticipate and mitigate potential triggers and reduce stress in the environment.

To do this well, it is important to gather meaningful input from the users of the space. If the specific clients or end users are not available for contact, we should research common characteristics or symptoms of similar groups and gather input from the staff who will be providing services and occupying the space.

Because inequities can be experienced as traumatic, TiD is inherently a form of social justice. In order for a project to be considered TiD, the architects or designers involved have a responsibility to identify, address, and, when possible, contribute to the dismantling and redressing of power imbalances through their work.

THE PRACTICE OF TRAUMA-INFORMED DESIGN

Trauma-informed Design is a practice. It is not a set of standards, and there is not a list of design approaches or features that can be applied to all projects—or even all projects of the same type—to make them TiD.

As with all practices, TiD requires practitioners to understand the concepts and theories relating to it, and to apply them to projects with fidelity. Because the goal is to anticipate and mitigate stressors and triggers in the environment, which we know are incredibly personal, TiD demands a customized approach to each and every project. The TiD Framework identifies three spheres and 11 domains to help practitioners focus their approach to this work, but they are not all-encompassing.

TiD practitioners distill information gathered from organizations, clients, and other invested parties to parse out what stressors exist, either as a result of past

CASE STUDY 1

Securing Possessions at a Shelter for Unhoused Youth

When designing a shelter for unhoused youth, the designers sought direct input from youth with lived experience. They learned many of the youth who would use the program had few possessions. As they had no permanent domicile, they often carried everything they owned with them, wherever they went. They were therefore very concerned about theft or loss.

TiD Response:

As the shelter was intended to provide a safe place for respite and rest, the design team recognized the importance of providing a way for residents to secure their belongings while they were at the shelter. As a direct response to the input received, the designers included lockers, in which the residents could store their possessions while they slept, refueled, and accessed services. By listening and responding to the input of youth with lived experience, the designers were able to optimize the design and create a space in which residents would not have to remain constantly vigilant, and could more readily engage in logical-thinking processes and control their reactions to situations. This simple design addition addressed a stressor previously faced by many residents.

CASE STUDY 2

- -

Searches Area in a Secure Correctional Facility

When designing a secure correctional facility, the architects focused on the types of things that happen in prisons and identified stressors that arose from the processes and interactions that occur regularly. One identified stressor was searches.

Individuals who are incarcerated are subject to various types of searches, including unclothed searches before, and after, receiving visits. These searches are extremely uncomfortable in the best of circumstances. As most correctional facilities are not built with searches in mind, however, they are often conducted in small corners or closet-like areas, with little privacy. Conducting searches in these conditions can contribute to the sense that the process is dehumanizing and lead those incarcerated to limit how often they participate in visits.

- -

TiD Response:

As the shelter was intended to provide In an effort to communicate a sense of worth and dignity, the architects designed a waiting room for individuals who are incarcerated, just outside the visiting room. In the back of this room, they added partitions similar to shower stalls, shielded from view by curtains. Individuals wait on sleek, wood benches in the open space until they are searched in an private stall. Once searched, they can pass through to the visiting room or back to the secure portion of the facility.

By thinking through the processes and interactions that occur regularly in correctional facilities, the architects identified that the location of where searches were being conducted increased the stress associated with visits. By proactively planning for a routine practice and providing a clean, well-lit space with biophilic features and enhanced privacy, they mitigated the stressor and created a more comfortable experience for individuals who are incarcerated. The goal of this approach was to increase the frequency of visits, thereby helping those incarcerated maintain ties with their family, friends, and community, which is a key indicator of successful reintegration.

CASE STUDY 3

Transitional Housing Program Intake Area for Survivors of Domestic Violence

When working on a project to move a secure, transitional housing program into a new space, the design team intended to locate the intake area directly inside the main entrance. It was planned to have floor-to-ceiling windows facing onto the sidewalk, and would be configured as an office containing a small seating area with a loveseat and another comfortable chair or two.

Trauma-Informed Understanding:

Survivors of domestic violence typically enter transitional housing programs immediately following a particularly violent episode. This means the intake process takes place while they are in crisis. They are sometimes injured and often afraid of being discovered. If they have children, they often arrive at the program with them, hoping for a safe place to gain their footing and plan their next steps.

Individuals who engage in abusive behavior often use threats to control their victims and make it hard for them to leave. This includes threatening to harm family members, loved ones, and pets. When they share children, the threats often include seeking sole custody and preventing the victim from being able to see their children.

During the intake, survivors are asked questions about the experiences that led them to seek assistance, are introduced to the program rules, and need to complete and sign binding agreements. It is a difficult and highly-emotional process, conducted at a time when they are experiencing high levels of stress.

TiD Response:

The TiD practitioners raised concerns about the location and design of the intake area. They explained that, to make survivors feel more safe after fleeing a dangerous home situation, the intake area should be moved further into the space, and away from the windows onto the street. This would make them feel further from reach, and shield them from being identified by passersby.

In addition, the intake area should only have one entrance, that can be clearly seen by the survivor throughout the intake process. Having more than one door into the intake area may leave survivors to feel exposed, and as though someone can inadvertently or intentionally enter at any time. Further, this space should not be directly connected to program space. Connecting the intake area to a program space increases >>

CASE STUDY 3 *(cont'd)*

the odds that someone may accidentally enter the space and could result in discussions being overheard. The intake area should be secluded from all other parts of the building, so incoming survivors feel protected and enclosed in safe surroundings.

Through their research, the TiD practitioners became aware that 70 percent of the program's residents were children. Based on this information, they advocated that the configuration of the intake room should also be rethought, to allow for parents to complete the intake process in a space with sound-separation from their children, but maintain an ability to see them. This visibility protects against unnecessary fears that the parent and child will be separated, while the sound-separation allows the parent to engage in the intake without concerns that the child will overhear a retelling of the situation or details that may be distressing and possibly triggering. Adding toys and children's books can help distract the children throughout the process.

experiences or the interactions that will occur in the space. They then find ways to mitigate those stressors through the design. This necessitates a keen listening awareness and ability, a highly developed skill of empathy, and an individualized approach to every project.

These three case studies illustrate how TiD can be used to address and mitigate potential stressors or triggers in the built environment.

THE THREE SPHERES OF THE TID FRAMEWORK

The work of TiD practitioners manifests primarily in three spheres: policy and practice; the design process; and the built environment. Each is equally important, and it is the TiD practitioner's responsibility to ensure that each aligns with the principles of trauma-informed care. If, in the course of a project, the practitioner identifies a concern with a particular policy, practice, process, or design element when viewed with a trauma-informed lens, they are expected to bring it to light and work with the appropriate parties to address it.

THE 11 DOMAINS OF THE TID FRAMEWORK

The TiD Framework offers 11 domains through which TiD practitioners can apply their understanding of the users and their unique needs, to develop a space that promotes safety, well-being, belonging, and healing. Each domain aligns with a SAMHSA principle of trauma-informed care, and is broken down into one or more key components.

As the key components apply across the three TiD spheres, the Framework outlines strategies that should be present in each sphere, followed by tactics. While not all the tactics need to be present, they serve as evidence that the key component is being met in that sphere.

The strategies and lists of tactics are not exhaustive, but serve as examples for practitioners, who may find other evidence of a key component in a project. Ideally, TiD practitioners should strive to meet as many tactics and strategies, of as many of the domains as possible, in each project.

Three Spheres and 11 Domains of Trauma-informed Design

Trauma-informed Design tends to each of the 11 domains in all three spheres: policy and practice, the design process, and the built environment.

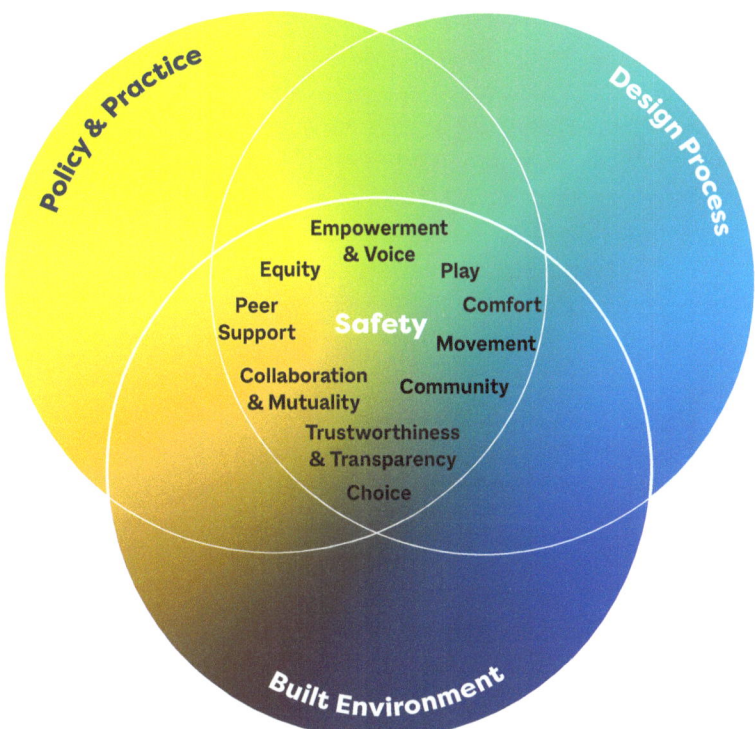

Figure 8. Three spheres and 11 domains of the TiD Framework

5

SPHERE 1:
POLICY AND PRACTICE

TO CREATE HEALING AND SAFE ENVIRONMENTS, IT IS IMPERATIVE THAT architects and designers ensure the policies and practices impacting users of the space are trauma-informed. This applies not only to the policies and practices of the design or architecture firm itself, but also to those of any organizations that provide services in the space.

No matter how health-centered, thoughtfully-created, and beautiful a building may be, it will not have the positive effects we are striving for if the people working, living, or receiving services in the space are being harmed by the practices in place. For this reason, TiD cannot, and should not, be separated from a trauma-informed approach throughout the organization, embedded in policy. SAMHSA takes a broad view of this, stating:

There are written policies and protocols establishing a trauma-informed approach as an essential part of the organizational mission. Organizational procedures and cross agency protocols, including working with community-based agencies, reflect trauma-informed principles. This approach must be "hard-wired" into practices and procedures of the organization, not solely relying on training workshops or a well-intentioned leader (SAMHSA, 2014).

It is fundamental that the trauma-informed practitioner makes it a part of their regular process to review the policies and practices of the organizations with which they work whenever possible, to ensure that they align with the principles of trauma-informed care. If they identify something that does not support this approach, they should call it to the attention of the organization and advocate for an effective change. This may take various forms, including:

* Making recommendations about policy and practice, along with clear explanations of the reasoning behind them;
* Working with the organization to identify alternative solutions; and
* Weaving recommendations into the ultimate design.

These conversations may seem uncomfortable at times, as they are outside the traditional scope of designers and architects. This is heightened by the fact that many of the clients seeking TiD services are educational, medical, mental health, and social service organizations, who in many ways, are the experts in the delivery of services. For similar reasons, some providers may resent this type of review and engagement from designers and architects.

Nonetheless, it is essential to the effectiveness of the built environment's ability to impact stress levels, and therefore essential to the TiD process, regardless of the type of organization. To ease any potentially difficult conversations with the organization, it is important to introduce the purpose of this part of the process early in the relationship-building phase with the client, as part of explaining how TiD services differ from a typical design process.

Engaging the client or organization in conversations at the beginning of the process can help reach a shared understanding of the purpose of TiD and introduce the processes the practitioner will use. Practitioners can explain that they conduct a review of the organization's policies and practices to better understand daily operations and identify anything that might be stress-inducing in the environment. They should let the client know they will use this information to provide mitigating strategies, and that all recommendations will be documented in writing, accompanied by the reason for the recommendation. This not only provides transparency, but also facilitates conversations about which recommendations to implement. Knowing why a specific recommendation is made, and the impact it could have on people in the space, can help clients better

It is fundamental that the trauma-informed practitioner makes it a part of their regular process to review the policies and practices of the organizations with which they work whenever possible, to ensure that they align with the principles of trauma-informed care.

TRAUMA-INFORMED DESIGN

assess whether they should adopt it.

Frequently, the organizations seeking TiD services have limited budgets and are constrained by the opinions of board members or public perception. This can present challenges in adopting trauma-informed approaches, especially when they include spending funds on design features viewed as luxuries. TiD practitioners have a responsibility to make organizations aware of all the known concerns and possible ways to redress them, then work with the client to identify the strongest approaches to achieve the desired outcomes of TiD within the known limitations of the project.

Having conversations that set these expectations at the start of the project can go a long way towards easing concerns when clients receive extensive recommendations. The client can rest assured that the practitioner will guide them in selecting the most effective, suitable approaches for their project.

There may also be times when the client or organization resists specific recommendations because they do not align with their views or established practices. In such cases, TiD practitioners should pay close attention to the client's response. Sometimes, there are other ways to address the client's concerns while implementing the recommendation. Providing suggestions as hypotheticals can sometimes make them easier to consider. Practitioners could try the wording, "How about [we try]…" to make these conversations feel more collaborative.

In cases when the client decides not to adopt a recommendation, the practitioner should document the reason. This level of documentation serves as a record for anyone reviewing the project of why decisions were made, and can help the practitioner look for alternatives in the future.

Just as it is important for clients to be open to feedback on their policies and practices, firms offering TiD services should welcome such input as well. Each of us views the world through the lens of our own life experiences, and as such, can never fully understand the way someone else views an event or situation, no matter how much we have in common with them. Being trauma-informed requires being open to others' points of view and using their input and feedback to continuously improve our process and approach.

CASE STUDY 4

Food Access at Transitional Housing Program for Survivors of Domestic Violence

When working on a project to move a transitional housing program for survivors of domestic violence into a new space, the TiD practitioners became aware that the program's staff regularly locked the pantries and refrigerators outside of specified meal preparation times, so residents could not access the food.

Trauma-Informed Understanding:

Survivors of domestic violence have often been worn down over time, and have had all control over their lives removed. Within abusive relationships, the individual with power often uses mechanisms of control that serve to isolate their victims and make it hard for them to leave the relationship. This often includes limiting food or its access. It is essential to their recovery that survivors be empowered to make decisions governing their own health and bodies.

Research also shows that food insecurity is an important risk indicator for intimate partner violence. As abusers rely on financial abuse to control their victims, many survivors have experienced difficulty obtaining sufficient, nutritious food.

The fact that 70% of the program's residents were children raised additional concerns. Children who grow up with food insecurity develop complicatedrelationships with food, and often need to learn how to identify and interpret their body-signals of hunger, satisfaction, and overeating so they can adopt healthy eating habits.

This is complicated by the fact that people who have high cortisol levels, such as those exposed to danger in their own homes, often experience false hunger signals, regardless of their age. They may repeatedly seek food and be unable to satiate their appetite.

In addition, food is intertwined with cultural identity: we come together over food; it plays a large part in our celebrations; we all have different styles of cooking that have been handed down or adopted, based on who we are and what we hold dear. Limiting access to food can further break-down these important aspects of survivors' sense of personal identity, and has a distressing and domineering impact over survivors.

During the intake, survivors are asked questions about the experiences that led them to seek assistance, are introduced to the program rules, and need to complete and sign binding agreements. It is a difficult and highly-emotional process, conducted at a time when they are experiencing high levels of stress. >>

TRAUMA-INFORMED DESIGN

CASE STUDY 4 *(cont'd)*

TiD Response:

Given their understanding of the dynamics of domestic violence and the impacts of trauma, the TiD consultants raised their concerns about locking away the food to the service provider. The service provider defended the practice, saying that, prior to the locks being installed, residents accessed the food at all hours, and although the program provided enough food to meet the daily requirements of all the residents, there were frequent shortages. These shortages created a significant impact on their budget, which were eliminated with the installation of the locks.

As the provider was not receptive to their initial inquiry, the TiD consultants addressed the concern more officially in their written recommendation report. They supported the recommendation that refrigerators, freezers, and pantries should not include locks, or be designed in a way that allowed for a lock to be added, with a full explanation of their reasoning and asserted that not being able to access food on demand has the opposite effect we strive for in trauma-informed care and design. In doing so, they made the provider aware of why the change was so important to the success of the project in a non-threatening manner. The provider was able to consider the consultants' reasoning in their own time and space, and come to the best solution for their program and residents.

6

SPHERE 2:
DESIGN PROCESS

T O AVOID CAUSING HARM, IT IS ESSENTIAL THAT THE PROCESSES TID partitioners use are trauma-informed. Traditional design processes include power imbalances that must be leveled to truly welcome, receive, and incorporate robust and substantial input from the community of users (Farkas, 2019).

Leveraging human-centered design (HCD) approaches enables TiD practitioners to work actively towards rebalancing the power dynamics of a traditional approach. HCD prioritizes the needs, perspectives, and experiences of the people who will use the design, or who are otherwise invested in its success, through direct interaction and empathy – not just at the onset of a project but iteratively throughout the design process and even after the design is installed. In the context of TiD, we use a broad understanding of who is considered an invested party, and include staff, contractors, partners, clients or customers, the general public, visitors, and end users.

With any design project, TiD practitioners are also faced with the constraints of budgets, timelines, and codes or other regulations. HCD provides a foundation to maintain the user perspective at the heart of the design while managing the need to address other project drivers. By iteratively involving users and reviewing in-progress designs with them, TiD practitioners can ensure that the translation of the design inputs and ideas from users matches their original intent.

As TiD is about the process and not just the final design, it is imperative that TiD practitioners document their process, including all recommendations, decision points, rationales, and outcomes. This allows for transparency and provides critical insight to others who may review the project at a later point in time.

HUMAN-CENTERED DESIGN

At the core of HCD is a deep understanding of invested parties' needs, emotions, and behaviors. Designers engage with invested parties to uncover insights that inform the development of solutions tailored to their unique contexts.

There are different types of HCD processes, depending on how much involvement invested parties have. Many traditional design processes involve designers and architects creating a space for users, with limited input and diminishing the complexity of humans into "users." There are very few projects that employ **user-generated design,** in which the design is created by the users (Dovetail Editorial Team, 2024). TiD generally involves **co-design,** in which the design is created with users. **Human-centered design** seeks to broaden the influence of "users," so they can inform the design based on all aspects of their lived experiences.

Research suggests that design activities that more actively engage invested parties results in more innovative design concepts and improved user satisfaction. By identifying design concerns early in the process, TiD practitioners face fewer surprises requiring them to reimagine already-approved designs, which saves in overall project costs (Dovetail Editorial Team, 2024; Interaction Design Foundation, 2024).

HCD aligns with the SAMSHA key principles of a trauma-informed approach, most notably by providing empowerment, voice, choice, and collaboration. The process is intended to identify and help mitigate potential stressors and triggers, enhancing users' sense of safety. The final design will more accurately reflect features of the community as a result of their participation. Ideally, survivors or participants can come together through the process, which provides an opportunity for peer support.

Foundational Principles of HCD

There are several key principles of HCD that are essential to a TiD project.

Collaboration and Human Focused

TiD processes include collaborative activities where participants can contribute their knowledge, insights, and ideas. They encourage the exchange of ideas and perspectives among diverse invested parties. This process of co-creation allows for a richer understanding of user-needs, enabling designers to develop more effective and relevant solutions. The collaboration can take various forms, such as workshops, interviews, brainstorming sessions, and co-design exercises (Cipan, 2023; Dovetail Editorial Team, 2024; Interaction Design Foundation, 2024).

Empathy and Contextual Understanding

Developing empathy and contextual understanding helps TiD practitioners put themselves in the users' shoes to understand their needs, desires, and challenges. This empathetic approach fosters a more human-centered process, leading to designs that better resonate with them and improve their overall experience (Cipan, 2023; Dam & Siang, 2024; Interaction Design Foundation, 2024).

TiD practitioners must listen to the participants to understand the context behind their feedback. Sometimes the feedback will be very specific to an individual or situation, and the practitioner must parse out what the main concern is and how to successfully address it in the environment. By paying attention to the cultural, social, and environmental factors of the users and project, practitioners can create solutions tailored to the specific context (Cipan, 2023; Dam & Siang, 2024; Interaction Design Foundation, 2024).

Inclusivity and Diversity

Inclusivity and diversity in the design process is an intentional effort to include as diverse a range of participants as possible in the process. It ensures a wide range of perspectives and experiences are considered during the design process, and leads to more accessible and inclusive solutions that cater to a broad user base, ultimately promoting equity and reducing potential barriers for groups of users (Cipan, 2023; Dovetail Editorial Team, 2024). To include a diverse group, TiD practitioners can reach out to underrepresented groups and use accessible meeting formats and culturally-sensitive facilitation methods.

Empowerment

TiD processes should encourage invested parties to actively influence design decisions. Their input and feedback must be valued and incorporated into the design process. This promotes empowerment, by giving users a voice in the design process. It also fosters a sense of ownership and investment in the final product, increasing user satisfaction and engagement (Cipan, 2023; Dovetail Editorial Team, 2024; Interaction Design Foundation, 2024).

Iteration and Adaptability

HCD, by its nature, contains a continuous feedback loop for improvement and refinement, based on participant feedback and insights. It also recognizes that users' needs and preferences may change over time.

TRAUMA-INFORMED DESIGN

Both participants and TiD practitioners have distinct roles. Participants should help evaluate ideas, drawings, and designs; provide feedback; and suggest improvements. Practitioners should remain open to change and willing to adapt based on evolving user requirements.

This approach enables TiD practitioners to identify and address potential issues or challenges early and often in the process, which can lead to more successful, less expensive solutions. Their final designs more effectively meet user-needs and remain relevant and valuable longer (Cipan, 2023; Dovetail Editorial Team, 2024; Interaction Design Foundation, 2024).

User Advocacy

It is a TiD practitioner's responsibility to empower participants to advocate for themselves throughout the design process. If participants seem unable or unwilling to engage, the practitioner must make adjustments to create an environment that encourages them to do so. TiD practitioners must address power imbalances and encourage participation. One way to achieve this is by prioritizing users' interests and goals in the design. The goal is to create an equitable and safe space for collaboration and co-design, so your end design creates a safe space for users (Interaction Design Foundation, 2024).

PARTICIPATORY DESIGN

Participatory design, which is sometimes referred to as "co-operative design," "co-design," or "community design," (Cipan, 2023; Dovetail Editorial Team, 2024; Elizarova & Dowd, 2023) is an essential feature of TiD. It is an HCD method that actively strives to involve all invested parties in the design process, to help ensure the result meets their needs, by applying their knowledge and experiences directly (Cipan, 2023; Dovetail Editorial Team, 2024; Elizarova & Dowd, 2023).

Participatory design is often seen as an important part of any design process because it helps with placekeeping, or highlighting a community's positive characteristics to bring vitality through design (see the section entitled Placekeeping for further details). In TiD, this process has an even more vital role because it helps us identify what specific types of features or situations might be stressful or triggering to those who will be using the space.

Practitioners may have clients who wish to limit participatory design. This may be because they fear it will slow the process or are concerned that the interests of other invested parties may not align with theirs. It is important that practitioners explain the benefits and reasons for using a participatory approach at the start of the project. Understanding that taking the time to gather and apply input from

Cautionary Tale 1:
Child Welfare Office

While working on a project for a child welfare agency, an architectural firm met with administrators of the agency to garner an understanding of what they were hoping for in the new space. They then held a focus group with staff and asked broad, open-ended questions intended to inform their design. These questions centered on the following topics:

* Their experiences with the existing physical space;
* Any "unique" requirements for their space;
* Any trauma-informed practices staff were using, of which the designers should be aware;
* Staff self-care spaces;
* The demographics of the families served by the agency;
* Physical safety concerns; and
* Features that staff felt could bring feelings of happiness, comfort, safety, support, growth, nurturing, affirmation, empowerment, and trust. When the service provider read the draft proposal, they rightfully called attention to the poor word choices and provided alternatives.

Having completed these conversations, they believed they were fairly well informed about how to design a trauma-informed space for the agency.

What Was Missed

The firm did not meet with, or elicit any feedback from, families served by the agency. As such, they did not comprehend the types of interactions that occur in the spaces, the trauma of being involved in the child welfare system, or the specific experiences or effects felt by families with such involvement. Without understanding their perspective, the firm could never adequately anticipate their stressors and possible triggers.

When Confidentiality Precludes Access to Clients

The main reason the firm did not involve families in its research was because the agency had to maintain their confidentiality. TiD practitioners often work with organizations that have a responsibility or mandate to protect the names and private information of their clients. To overcome this, they need to find ways to gather information while protecting the privacy of these clients. Understanding of these topics, they would have been much better informed to provide TiD services for the agency.

They could have then begun the process of identifying stressors and possible triggers. They could have also then asked the agency to facilitate an anonymous survey of the families being served, to gain feedback >>

TRAUMA-INFORMED DESIGN

directly from the families and refine their assumptions. With the proper clinical support and strict parameters around the types of topics included, they may have even been able to arrange for double-blind interviews if more input was needed. The firm also could have recruited individuals who have used similar services or otherwise represent this population by partnering with a research recruitment agency or non-profit advocacy organization.

To start, the firm in this example should have conducted background research into the child welfare system and how it operates. If they had fully engaged in Sphere I, and reviewed the agency's policies, they would have formed at least a partial understanding that could then have been supplemented by other resources about the impacts of childhood abuse and neglect and witnessing domestic violence. With a deeper understanding of these topics, they would have been much better informed to provide TiD services for the agency.

They could have then begun the process of identifying stressors and possible triggers. They could have also then asked the agency to facilitate an anonymous survey of the families being served, to gain feedback directly from the families and refine their assumptions. With the proper clinical support and strict parameters around the types of topics included, they may have even been able to arrange for double-blind interviews if more input was needed. The firm also could have recruited individuals who have used similar services or otherwise represent this population by partnering with a research recruitment agency or non-profit advocacy organization.

invested parties can prevent impractical outcomes that counter the TiD principles, can help with client buy-in. As with any TiD recommendation, if the client rejects or overly-restricts a participatory design process, practitioners should document this as part of the overall design documentation.

PHASES OF THE DESIGN PROCESS

In an HCD process enriched with trauma-informed principles, users are actively involved at every stage. Each phase not only centers on creating solutions but also ensures users feel safe, empowered, respected, genuinely cared for, and supported. By inviting users to co-design their experiences, designers foster solutions that align with both practical needs and emotional well-being, creating a supportive, restorative design.

Here's how each step integrates user-participation and trauma-informed practices:

1. Empathize

Designers start by conducting in-depth, empathetic research to understand the users' experiences, challenges, and needs, especially if they've experienced trauma. Research methods such as interviews, observations, or workshops are approached with sensitivity, using open, non-intrusive questions and safe, comfortable environments. Designers aim to build trust and acknowledge the power dynamics in these interactions. Trauma-informed principles like safety, choice, and transparency guide these interactions, helping users feel secure, heard, and respected throughout.

2. Define

In this phase, designers work closely with users to distill findings into a problem statement. Synthesizing user insights, designers focus on identifying core needs and prioritize user safety, choice, and control in problem framing. Designers may hold collaborative sessions with users, sharing summaries and engaging them in defining their needs and refining the problem statement together. Trauma-informed language is used to avoid re-traumatization, ensuring that the problem statement reflects users' perspectives accurately and respectfully.

3. Ideate

Ideation is a highly collaborative step where users are invited to co-create possible solutions. Designers facilitate inclusive brainstorming sessions, encouraging users to share ideas without judgment. Trauma-informed principles play a critical role here: designers ensure that participants feel empowered, set boundaries comfortably, and choose their level of involvement. Ideation tools, like storyboards or role-playing, help visualize ideas, offering users a safe way to envision solutions that address their needs without triggering negative responses.

4. Prototype

During prototyping, designers develop early, tangible versions of solutions, creating an open feedback loop with users. To incorporate trauma-informed principles, designers might create multiple low-stakes options, allowing users to provide input without feeling pressured. Designers engage users to test these early versions in safe environments and are transparent about how their feed-

TRAUMA-INFORMED DESIGN

back will inform iterations. Users are encouraged to share honest opinions, and adjustments are made in ways that protect their emotional comfort and control.

5. Test

Testing is a collaborative phase where users interact directly with prototypes, and designers observe and gather feedback. This step prioritizes user consent and comfort by making testing environments welcoming and non-intimidating. Trauma-informed testing strategies may include providing users with options to stop or modify their participation at any time. Designers remain mindful of potential triggers and ensure users feel safe and in control, respecting boundaries while making necessary adjustments based on users' insights.

6. Implement

In the implementation phase, users remain integral, as their feedback is essential to successful roll-out and long-term use. Designers can provide ongoing check-ins, allowing users to share how the final solution impacts their lives and whether it continues to meet their needs. This stage supports a feedback loop that empowers users to voice adjustments they may need over time, ensuring the design adapts to any evolving needs in a trauma-informed, supportive way.

ETHICAL CONSIDERATIONS

Developing a strong understanding of the community that will use the space is essential to TiD. To achieve this goal, TiD practitioners create an atmosphere that feels safe to the participants, reflects their dignity, shows their input is valued, and provides them with respect and closure.

In TiD research, ethical considerations are not just a set of rules but a continuous practice of sensitivity, awareness, and reflexivity. Central to this practice is a deep respect for participants, who may have experienced significant trauma, making them more vulnerable in research settings. This respect is grounded in the Belmont Report's principles: respect for persons, beneficence, and justice (Sims, 2010).

Respect for persons emphasizes the importance of autonomy and informed consent, ensuring that participants fully understand their role and the risks involved, and that they willingly participate. When relying on input from marginalized communities or vulnerable participants, it is essential that we are mindful that sharing their personal stories and feelings may have a toll, and provide sufficient supports (Dietkus, 2022). Researchers should be diligent in offering clear, transparent, and reliable communication throughout the process, avoiding any form of coercion or manipulation.

The principle of beneficence requires that the practitioner maximizes potential benefits while minimizing harm. This is particularly critical in TiD, where the very act of asking someone to recount their experiences could trigger emotional distress. Practitioners should strive to create environments that are physically, emotionally, and psychologically safe, and be prepared to offer resources or referrals for mental health support if needed. A trauma-informed

To achieve this goal, TiD practitioners create an atmosphere that feels safe to the participants, reflects their dignity, shows their input is valued, and provides them with respect and closure.

approach necessitates not only the prevention of harm but also the active promotion of healing and empowerment through the design process.

Justice demands that the benefits and burdens of research be distributed equitably. Historically, this principle has often been violated, as marginalized communities have frequently borne the brunt of exploitative research practices. The infamous Tuskegee Syphilis Study, in which African American men were misled and denied treatment (Brandt 1978), and the unauthorized use of Henrietta Lacks' cells without her consent (Skloot, 2017), exemplify profound breaches of ethical conduct that disproportionately harmed vulnerable populations. Such cases reveal how research, when not conducted ethically, can reinforce systemic inequalities. TiD seeks to break from this past by engaging diverse participants and making their voices central to the design process. It acknowledges that those who have experienced trauma bring invaluable insights into the creation of spaces and systems that can promote healing and resilience.

Research Risk-Management

When engaging in trauma-informed design research, identifying potential risks to participants is an essential component of ethical practice. Trauma-affected individuals often carry heightened sensitivities, making them more vulnerable to emotional distress, re-traumatization, or harm during the research process. Therefore, TiD practitioners should do their best to emulate design researchers and try to anticipate and mitigate these risks to protect participants' well-being. Recognizing and addressing risks not only adheres to ethical research standards but also helps to build trust with participants, ensuring they feel safe and respected throughout the study.

TRAUMA-INFORMED DESIGN

Every stage of research—design, data collection, analysis, and dissemination—should be scrutinized for potential threats to participants' mental and emotional health. This process goes beyond the basic assessment of physical risks to include emotional, psychological, and relational factors that could exacerbate trauma responses. For example, discussing traumatic experiences or recalling distressing memories can trigger flashbacks, anxiety, or emotional upheaval. If these risks are not carefully identified and managed, participants may suffer unnecessary harm, undermining the ethical integrity of the study.

To effectively identify risks, trauma-informed research should incorporate a collaborative and reflexive approach. This begins with conducting a thorough risk assessment during the research design phase, where researchers must anticipate possible adverse reactions based on the nature of the trauma being studied and the vulnerabilities of the participant population. Consulting with trauma experts, mental health professionals, and invested parties from the community can provide valuable insights into potential triggers and how to mitigate them. Additionally, involving participants in the research design process can reveal unanticipated risks, ensuring the study is sensitive to the real needs and concerns of the target group. By adopting a proactive and participatory approach, researchers can better protect participants, promote ethical integrity, and contribute to the creation of trauma-sensitive research settings where healing and empowerment are prioritized.

A key strategy in identifying risks is pilot testing. Running a small-scale version of the activity can help researchers observe how participants respond to questions, topics, or stimuli that could evoke emotional distress. This allows the TiD team to adjust their methods, wording, or timing to avoid triggering trauma responses. Pilot testing also helps to identify any gaps in the available support systems for participants, such as immediate access to mental health resources or strategies for self-regulation during or after the study.

Informed consent processes are another vital tool in risk management. When participants are fully informed about the nature of the study, including the potential risks, they can provide consent based on a clear understanding of what their involvement entails. This transparency fosters an open dialogue, allowing participants to voice any concerns or suggest ways to modify the research to better suit their needs. TiD practitioners must remain flexible and responsive, adjusting their methods as new risks are identified during the course of the activity.

Reflexivity

Addressing bias in research is another critical component of ethical TiD. Bias, whether conscious or unconscious, can shape the questions practitioners ask, the data they collect, and how they interpret findings.

To combat bias and power imbalances, TiD research must be reflexive. Reflexivity involves a continual process of self-awareness, where practitioners critically examine their assumptions, positionality, and potential blind spots. It means acknowledging how their social, cultural, and professional backgrounds may shape the design process and outcomes. This self-awareness is vital when working with trauma-affected populations, as it helps practitioners recognize and mitigate the ways in which their own power and privilege might influence engagement by invested parties or the interpretation of data. Reflexivity fosters a more ethical, participatory environment, where participants are viewed not merely as subjects but as co-creators of knowledge.

Reflexive processes also allow TiD practitioners to learn and adapt as their work evolves. Ethical TiD and research involves constant feedback loops, where the methods, interactions, and even the designs themselves are adjusted in response to the needs and feedback of participants. This iterative approach honors the lived experiences of those involved and ensures that the process maintains its integrity by continuously aligning with ethical standards. Additionally, it demonstrates a commitment to the integrity of research, ensuring that findings are valid, credible, and genuinely reflective of the diverse voices and experiences of participants.

A lack of diversity in TiD teams can further exacerbate this, leading to narrow, incomplete understandings of trauma and its impacts. TiD must prioritize inclusion and diversity at every level—researchers, designers, participants, and invested parties. Ensuring that people from diverse cultural, racial, and socioeconomic backgrounds are included not only broadens the scope of understanding but also helps avoid the perpetuation of stereotypes or misrepresentations of certain groups.

TRAUMA-INFORMED RESEARCH PRACTICES

There are many different types of research and co-design activities TiD practitioners can incorporate (Elizarova & Dowd, 2023). They can get creative with this, and it can be quite fun. The key is that the activity should be designed to elicit the information needed to build the best environment for the participants—one in which they will feel safe, supported, comfortable, and empowered.

When working with individuals who may have experienced trauma, TiD practitioners have a responsibility to ensure their practices and approach are trauma-informed. Before starting a participatory design session, TiD practitioners should thoughtfully plan it in a way that is structured, includes the right participants, and successfully elicits the information needed. This includes ensuring the room is set up to be welcoming and comfortable and that staff use open body language

TRAUMA-INFORMED DESIGN

(e.g., smiling; uncrossing arms and legs; using hand gestures; raising eyebrows; tilting head; maintaining eye contact, if it is well-received). To reduce the likelihood of misunderstandings and allow for honest, meaningful conversation, practitioners should arrange for interpreters if necessary. Additionally, practitioners should consider a variety of ways to elicit input and enable participation by all. For instance, practitioners can give participants options for how to provide their feedback on a design, such as live discussion and asynchronous worksheets completed after the session. Providing options empowers participants to participate in a way that aligns with their social interaction and disclosure preferences.

The practitioner should be as transparent as possible throughout the process. They should explain the reason for seeking feedback, what they are hoping to gain, and what the participant's involvement would entail. Will it be just one meeting, or multiple? How long will each meeting be? Will there be group activities or one-on-one interviews?

Transparency should extend to limitations, both throughout the process and at its conclusion. TiD practitioners should always review the design with participants and, if feedback was received and not incorporated into the design, explain why they were unable or unwilling to do so.

General Approach and Logistics

Each research or participatory activity follows the general steps outlined below (Dovetail Editorial Team, 2024):

Step 1: Define Goals

Defining goals helps TiD practitioners identify the purpose of involving participants in an activity, which in turn enables participants to know what is expected of them. This allows practitioners to focus on priority topics, reducing the potential of over-recruiting or otherwise asking too much of vulnerable participants. Having focused goals can reduce stress participants may feel about the day's events and what might be asked of them.

Step 2: Set Up Structure

Create a clear framework for the project, indicating how the proposed activities and methods align with the project purpose and research goals. The framework should also include timelines and milestones to facilitate logistical planning. By understanding how the research fits into the overall project milestones, TiD practitioners can better apply findings to the design solution.

The overall schedule should allow for cancellations, rescheduling, and other challenges. Practitioners should recognize that participants may experience work or family conflicts, transportation difficulties, or other complications, and ensure enough of a buffer in the schedule to allow full participation despite these disruptions.

Step 3: Recruit Participants

It is important to have the right people at the table. Participants should either be the expected users of the space or represent them as closely as possible; if more than one end user of the space exists, such as staff and clients, all should be included. Be sure to include users from any other applicable groups or invested parties as well.

In instances where expected users cannot be included, it is helpful to identify specific attributes of those users that enable TiD practitioners to understand how "proxy" participants represent the expected end users and how they are different. As a result, practitioners can identify limitations in the findings and seek alternative ways to validate or otherwise capture more direct inputs from the expected end users.

Step 4: Create a Detailed Plan

When planning TiD activities, practitioners should ensure good time management. They should allot enough time for the planned activities, so that participants know what their commitment is, and that activities stay on schedule. By planning more time for activities than believed necessary, it allows for adjustments due to participants' varying levels of ability and enables the practitioner to clarify instructions and accommodate requests for support. (Cipan, 2023; Dovetail Editorial Team, 2024). It is important to recognize that participants likely have other commitments, possibly including work or care-taking responsibilities, and that they could experience negative consequences if the process runs over the pre-scheduled time.

The schedule should include breaks, and participants should be encouraged to step out if necessary. If there is no set schedule, facilitators should offer them throughout the session. If possible, TiD practitioners should arrange for an additioal, separate space that individuals can use to self-soothe or regulate if necessary.

TiD practitioners should also proactively and repeatedly seek accommodation requests. These requests can be sought at multiple points in the research process, such as during recruitment, as part of scheduling reminders, and during the session itself. By seeking requests more than once, practitioners can capture a breadth of needs that can vary person-to-person or even for the same person day-to-day. Practitioners must follow through on their commitment to providing accommodations in order to demonstrate trust to participants. Therefore, they should be

TRAUMA-INFORMED DESIGN

careful not to overpromise what they can feasibly provide and be transparent if they are unable to meet specific requests.

Step 5: Conduct the Session or Activity

After the preparation, TiD practitioners should focus on the key principles of trauma-informed interviewing and moderating. First and foremost, they should ensure a culturally-responsive approach and build rapport and trust with participants. Throughout the session, they should watch for signs that a participant may have difficulty in understanding or due to the conversation itself, then address the need as soon as possible.

Facilitators play an important role. From the participant's perspective, their main goals are creating a safe and engaging atmosphere, encouraging ideas, time-keeping, and redirecting conversations when necessary. Perhaps their most important role, however, is observing participants, including their non-verbal language, for signs that they might be struggling (Dovetail Editorial Team, 2024), and supporting them, or connecting them to someone else who can do so. For this reason, it is often advisable that the facilitator be a separate person from the architect or designer, and be specifically trained in how to facilitate group activities in a trauma-informed manner.

To ensure key take-aways from the session are not lost, it is important that sessions be recorded. As audio or video recording may present safety or privacy concerns, it is often preferable that this be in the form of written notes. Whenever relying on written notes, it is recommended that notes be taken by both designers and facilitators, to ensure nothing is missed from either perspective (Dovetail Editorial Team, 2024). Some activities can also involve participants as notetakers or record their input through mapping activities (Elizarova & Dowd, 2023).

When conducting research or participatory design activities, tolerate pauses, even long ones. People will often speak to fill the silence if you let it continue long enough. TiD practitioners should ask questions that are relevant to understanding how participants experience the space but do so in a way that follows the natural course of conversation. For example, when interviewing residents of a transitional housing facility, the practitioner may want to ask about the facility rules or when, and where, they entertain visitors. Try not to interrupt someone while they are telling their story, and be sure to allow space, and enough time, for storytelling. It is often from these shared personal experiences that TiD practitioners can gather the most valuable information.

TiD practitioners should not push on difficult topics the first time they meet with a participant. After that, they should only revisit the topic if it is directly tied to their understanding of how that participant would react to the built environment.

As the session closes, TiD practitioners should thank participants for their time and the information they shared. Practitioners should provide participants with contact information, in case they think of more information they want to share. Before leaving, participants should be informed about the next phase of the project, and when, or if, they will be contacted again.

Step 6: Analyze and Report

In trauma-informed research, data analysis prioritizes sensitive, non-judgmental language that honors participants' experiences without dehumanizing or oversimplifying. TiD practitioners should avoid clinical jargon and instead use framing that respects each individual's unique responses to trauma, highlighting resilience and agency. This careful wording ensures findings convey empathy and respect, minimizing the risk of re-traumatization for readers or participants revisiting the data. A collaborative approach, such as member-checking, can strengthen the integrity of findings. By involving participants in reviewing and validating interpretations, researchers ensure that insights genuinely reflect participants' perspectives. This step not only adds credibility but also empowers participants, allowing them input on how their experiences are represented.

Recognizing the diverse ways individuals respond to trauma, trauma-informed analysis avoids universal conclusions. Instead, it acknowledges complexity, especially relevant to design solutions, where flexible and personalized approaches are key. Findings should clearly convey these nuances, informing design recommendations that are adaptable rather than prescriptive.

Following analysis, findings should be documented in a report. The report should include clear, respectful language, and each finding or recommendation should indicate the domain(s) of the TiD Framework with which it associates. This structure aligns the report with trauma-informed goals, offering readers a compassionate, well-rounded understanding of how design can support healing. The report should also include any limitations to the research or participatory approach. Limitations include factors or conditions that restrict the scope, validity, or generalizability of research findings. Recognizing these limitations is crucial for contextualizing results, guiding future research, and transparently acknowledging and mitigating potential influence on the results.

Step 7: Follow Up with Participants

Show participants the results of your analysis and any design concepts or solutions stemming from the activity, explaining how their feedback informed it. Then, ask for their feedback on the outputs, and use that to inform revisions.

By providing follow-up with participants, TiD practitioners are demonstrating

TRAUMA-INFORMED DESIGN

a commitment to participants and respecting the trust that participants placed in them. As part of the follow-up, practitioners should also be transparent about any feedback that could not be incorporated into the design and why.

IMPORTANCE OF LANGUAGE

The way we communicate with and about people reveals—and shapes—attitudes and behaviors. The language we use can alienate those with invaluable insight and contribute to stigmas, or it can signal respect and dignity.

It is important to use inclusive language at all times. Some general guidelines include:

* Using "person-first" language;
* Using gender-neutral language;
* Asking individuals how they identify;
* Asking individuals what their pronouns are, and using them;
* Using language that recognizes individuals' strengths; and
* Using an individual's or group's preferred language, even if it differs from these guidelines, provided it does not cause others harm.

There are a few keys to speaking in a respectful, trauma-informed way. The first is to remember that the individual, and their worth, is separate and distinct from their behavior, and that risky or criminalized behavior is often a trauma response. Because we understand that trauma responses are normal biological responses to abnormal events, trauma-informed practitioners actively shift their language from describing an individual by their behavior, abilities, or traits.

To ensure language is trauma-informed, TiD practitioners should always seek to replace language that dehumanizes with language that emphasizes the humanity of the individual, and to use language that is non-judgmental and normalizing. Avoid ableist and moralistic language, as well as language that is stigmatizing, perpetuates negative stereotypes or biases, is discriminatory, refers to people by a legal status, or has violent or racist connotations or historical meanings.

Below are some examples of how we can rephrase our language using these principles:

* When talking about substance use and mental health disorders and treatment, focus on the medical nature. An example of this is using "individual with a substance use disorder" rather than "drug abuser," "addict," "druggie," or "junkie."
* Focus on the behavior, which we recognize as a response or adaptation to an untenable situation, rather than the disorder or pathology. This would include using the phrase "individual affected by (or

engaging in) drug use." Another example is "individual with high-risk behavior."

* Shift the emphasis from pathology and suffering to resilience and healing. Rather than saying a person is "suffering" from a disease, say they are "living with" or "have" the disease. Similarly, a person did not "suffer" a traumatic event, they "experienced" or "survived" it.

Shifting to trauma-informed language takes time, as it is different from the pervasive language that surrounds us. TiD practitioners becoming familiar with speaking in person-first, neutral or positive language may find the social work adage, "speak to someone as if their mother is on one shoulder, and their lawyer is on the other" useful in the transition. Mistakes will happen, often due to the speed of conversation or lapses of awareness or memory. When these happen, we recommend providing yourself some grace, as we are all at different stages of learning. If someone points out the mistake, TiD practitioners should thank them for calling attention to it, apologize for any harm caused, and state that they will do their best to use the proper term going forward. If a practitioner recognizes the mistake themself, they can take a similar approach by apologizing and making an increased effort to remember in the future. In either case, if someone was harmed, the TiD practitioner should not expect or prompt the harmed individual to express forgiveness or comfort them in any way.

In addition to using trauma-informed language, TiD practitioners should remain mindful that a person may not be comfortable with disclosing certain aspects of their identity, and they should always support each individual's comfort and choice in this matter.

As the main objective of communication in the design process is to gain a better understanding of other's perspectives and experiences, it is also important to minimize the chance of misunderstandings. Slang, jargon, idioms, acronyms, and analogies all assume a shared understanding or experience to convey meaning. By avoiding their use, we can communicate more effectively.

For more examples of trauma-informed language, see Appendix A.

PERSONAL DISCLOSURES

TiD practitioners should be prepared for disclosures of a very personal nature. It is not uncommon for individuals to share personal accounts describing their traumatic experiences in this type of setting. When this happens, the primary role of the TiD practitioner is to preserve the sense of safety of participants.

If someone shares a disturbing account, the practitioner should thank them for sharing their story. Be compassionate, but matter-of-fact, about incidents of abuse or violence. Practitioners may wish to express their sorrow at the fact the individual had that experience, and acknowledge how difficult it must have been. It is important that practitioners try not to show their own discomfort or feelings, as the individual who disclosed may feel obligated to take care of the practitioner, or protect them from their stories.

At the same time, TiD practitioners need to be aware that others hearing the conversation, or they, themselves, may be affected or triggered by it. They should remain aware of their body signals and take a break or ask another practitioner to take over when necessary. If possible, it is helpful to have clinical support or extra facilitators available that can respond to individuals affected by others' stories while the group or activity continues. Additionally, practitioners can schedule breaks in between sessions to allow space and time to process their own emotions and responses to discussing difficult topics.

DYSREGULATION OF PARTICIPANTS

TiD practitioners should always keep an eye out for signs that participants may be becoming overwhelmed or agitated by the conversation. Signs of dysregulation may include: becoming silent; changing the subject; showing signs of extreme tiredness, confusion, or dissociation (e.g., as though they are on "autopilot" or floating through interactions); talking about the past in present terms; being non-responsive to direct communication; displaying signs of agitation or anger; or fidgeting or unrestrained moving.

If a practitioner recognizes that someone is becoming dysregulated, they should stop the conversation, and try to help the individual regulate. This can include having a clinician or facilitator step in, removing them to a separate regulatory space, or guiding them through some breathing exercises or mindfulness activities. Practitioners may also want to ask if there is anything they can do to help the individual feel more comfortable or safe. As individuals who are dysregulated may have a hard time understanding or responding, visual cues can help with communication.

TiD Practitioners should always remember that creating and preserving a sense of safety is paramount to a trauma-informed approach, and that our personal experiences factor into how safe a situation feels. Each person is their own gauge of safety, and when that is breached, it needs to be restored as soon as possible. Therefore, it does not matter if we, as professionals, believe the situation is safe if the participant does not feel safe themselves.

If the person starts to experience acute distress, contact local behavioral or mental health specialists or a national helpline for support and guidance on next steps.

Cautionary Tale 2:
Transitional Program for Individuals Who Are Unhoused

When trying to secure grant funding to cover the TiD consultation services for a project, the consultants used several poor word choices in their proposal. The project intended to repurpose a discontinued youth forensic facility as a living space and training center for men who were experiencing homelessness. Facing a strict word count limit, the consultants wrongfully opted for brevity rather than employing trauma-informed language, including inappropriately using:

✳ "Homeless" rather than "people experiencing homelessness" or "unhoused;"

✳ "Prison" or "jail" rather than "correctional facility;" and

✳ "Congregate living facility" and "congregate shelter," which have a negative connotation and imply a dormitory-style, provisional response to temporary and acute housing needs, rather than "single room occupancy housing."

When the service provider read the draft proposal, they rightfully called attention to the poor word choices and provided alternatives.

TiD Response

In response to this feedback, the consultants promptly edited the draft with more appropriate language and sent the revised proposal with an apology for any harm caused. This approach ensured that the relationship with the service provider remained strong despite the mistake in language choice.

TRANSLATING RESEARCH INTO DESIGNS

Integrating human-centered and trauma-informed approaches in design relies on continually connecting user insights back to the design solution itself. The objective is not simply to collect data but to shape every decision around the people who will interact with the final space or product. This connection to design means ensuring that insights on user-needs, particularly for those impacted by trauma, translate into features that directly address their emotional, physical, and psychological require-ments. Whether in spatial layouts, material selections, or lighting, every design element is an opportunity to reflect an understanding of the user, creating spaces that offer comfort, agency, and healing. This connection emphasizes the purpose of each design feature, reinforcing the intention to support user well-being.

Creating this connection begins by mapping out how each design element will

TRAUMA-INFORMED DESIGN

Cautionary Tale 3:
Trauma-informed Policing Conversation

While conducting a session on trauma-informed policing with a group of legal-system professionals, the material prompted a participant to recognize, for the first time, that an experience she had with a police officer was racially charged. Thinking she was positively contributing to the conversation, she disclosed the incident and told her story. In doing so, she clearly became triggered and other participants experienced negative reactions, ranging from discomfort to dysregulation.

TiD Response
The TiD consultant very quickly appointed someone to take over facilitating the conversation with the group and moved the woman to a private area. With the help of two other professionals, the consultant was able to provide support and help the woman to regulate. After telling her story, and explaining how she now realized it impacted many of her experiences since, she acknowledged the experience with the officer was traumatic, and expressed the desire to further process the event with the help of a clinician. The situation was positively resolved, without causing any further harm, but highlights the importance of a quick response and having extra support available when facilitating these types of conversations.

directly address the unique emotional, physical, and psychological needs of invested parties. TiD practitioners need to continually ask, "How does this decision serve the well-being of end users and other invested parties?" This commitment transforms data from abstract information into concrete design strategies that honor the lived experiences of trauma-affected individuals. The process of continuously anchoring design features to user-needs creates spaces and products that not only meet functional demands but also offer users a sense of control, calm, and healing.

Maintaining Diverse Perspectives
To foster designs that are genuinely inclusive and sensitive to trauma, TiD teams should reflect a diversity of backgrounds, perspectives, and lived experiences. Trauma is multifaceted, with individuals experiencing and processing it in deeply personal ways shaped by cultural, social, and economic factors. Having team members from varied backgrounds allows for richer empathy and a more holistic understanding of the potential needs of invested parties. Diverse teams are better equipped to notice subtle aspects of design that may be challenging or trigger-

ing for specific groups, promoting inclusivity from the ground up. This also allows for more robust discussions and a broader range of creative solutions, as different perspectives highlight biases, challenge assumptions, and uncover potential oversights. Building a culture of inclusion within the TiD team means that each member brings their unique lens to problem-solving, increasing the likelihood of developing solutions that respect the complexities of trauma, are more empathetic to diverse experiences of trauma, and resonate with a broader range of invested parties.

Flexible Thinking

Flexibility in the design process requires TiD practitioners to approach problem-solving through both divergence and convergence. In divergence, teams think expansively, exploring multiple ideas and interpretations of how a trauma-informed solution could take shape. This open-minded thinking is crucial for identifying possibilities that might not be obvious at first glance, helping teams consider unconventional solutions. Convergence, in turn, focuses on narrowing down options based on feasibility and alignment with invested parties, refining them into viable design concepts.

Each person is their own gauge of safety, and when that is breached, it needs to be restored as soon as possible. Therefore, it does not matter if we, as professionals, believe the situation is safe if the participant does not feel safe themselves.

TRAUMA-INFORMED DESIGN

A cycle of divergence and convergence can exist throughout the overall TiD process as ideas are updated in response to interactions with invested parties and reviewed against user-needs, codes and regulations, and project goals. This cyclical approach helps TiD practitioners balance creativity with practicality, enabling teams to iterate and refine ideas in a way that both honors user-needs and meets project constraints.

Differentiating Between Needs and Design Possibilities

A key part of a TiD process is clearly distinguishing between users' core needs and the range of design possibilities that could address them. While user-needs might include feelings of safety, control, and comfort, the ways to achieve these feelings in design can vary greatly. User-needs must remain consistent throughout the process, acting as a "north star" to guide decision-making. For example, creating a sense of security might involve adding visual privacy features but could also be achieved by developing quiet zones or implementing a circular layout that avoids hidden corners. However, at the root of each of these design elements is the user need to experience a feeling of security and safety.

Regularly checking that proposed solutions align with underlying needs is essential to avoid features that might detract from, rather than support, the user's experience. This alignment helps maintain focus, ensuring that each design choice remains grounded in actual user-needs rather than diverging into features that, while interesting, don't directly contribute to user well-being or risk becoming sources of unintentional stress.

User-Advocacy

TiD practitioners act as advocates for users throughout the journey from concept to implementation. Advocacy means consistently defending design decisions that support users' emotional and physical safety, even when compromises arise from budget, timeline, or preferences from other invested parties. It also involves championing the users' voice, ensuring their needs are forefront in every conversation. This advocacy role fosters a relationship of trust and accountability between designers and users, bridging the gap between user intent and final output and enabling designers to act as ethical stewards of users' needs and voices.

Decision-Tracking

An audit trail, or documentation that tracks design decisions, is crucial to the TiD process, offering a clear record of how user insights influenced the final solution. By documenting why and how certain user-needs were prioritized—and noting where adjustments or compromises occurred—designers provide an accessible narrative of the project's development. This traceability fosters transparency and accountability, showing how specific insights directly informed key design choices and where the team opted for alternative approaches. For example, if certain user suggestions couldn't be accommodated due to structural limitations or cost, an audit trail documents these constraints, maintaining clarity about the decision-making process. Traceability also supports iterative improvements post-implementation, providing a baseline that designers can return to for future modifications. This approach reinforces the trustworthiness of the design process, ensuring that users and other invested parties understand the rationale behind each decision and feel confident that their insights were considered, respected, and thoughtfully integrated.

PLACEKEEPING

In design, placemaking is an approach to strategically shaping and changing the physical and social character of a neighborhood, often including arts and cultural aspects. It is intended to be a collaborative process that seeks to strengthen the connection of community members to the places they share. Although some place-making processes are human-centered and emphasize the physical, cultural, and social identities of the community, the very concept of placemaking presupposes that the existing community and its spaces need outside assistance to improve.

The preferred alternative to placemaking is placekeeping, which builds on the strengths of the existing community. According to the U.S. Department of Arts and Culture, placekeeping is:

> ...the active care and maintenance of a place and its social fabric by the people who live and work there. It is not just preserving buildings but keep-ing the cultural memories associated with a locale alive, while supporting the ability of local people to maintain their way of life as they choose (Yu et al., 2018).

The placekeeping approach focuses on elevating the existing assets of a commu-nity, rather than reinventing it. As such, it is a way to resist neighborhood gentrifi-cation and the displacement that comes with it. Frequently, placekeeping efforts are led by community leaders with long roots in the area (ioby, 2023)

When providing TiD services, practitioners should consider how they can ampli-fy existing community resources to enhance the ability of community co-care through the project (see the Community Care section for more information on this concept). The first step is to assess the community and built environment, including the infrastructure, development, community organizations, and available services. The purpose of the assessment is twofold: to discover existing organiza-tions and services that could support the intended end users of the project and to identify any communal gaps that could potentially be filled by the project. With this information, the TiD practitioner can then determine the best way to foster opportunities for the community to engage with the users of the space, within the appropriate boundaries of the program.

As an example, consider the design of a new affordable housing development. By including public parking, meeting spaces, a day care center, employment services office, café, library, or public gym into the design, the developers can invite commu-nity members into the space. This can enhance the neighborhood's services while also fostering opportunities for more genuine interactions between the building's residents and other community members, which can grown into new, supportive

TRAUMA-INFORMED DESIGN

relationships. The development could grow into a meeting point and cultural center for the neighborhood by elevating its residents and providing a safe place for them to come together and support one another.

If the project were a transitional home for individuals who had experienced violence, however, it may not be appropriate for community members to enter the program site. In such cases, the TiD practitioner may consider whether they can support opportunities for residents to connect with the community outside the program or at another location.

SPHERE 3:
BUILT ENVIRONMENT

I N ADDITION TO ADDRESSING POLICY, PRACTICE, AND THE DESIGN PROCESS through Sphere I and II, the TiD practitioner considers the tools they will employ to create the built environment. This is where designers and architects can leverage their deep understanding of design principles and how different elements can influence a person's perception of the space. The skillful application of concepts such as effective lighting, visibility, acoustics, wayfinding, and biophilia can make significant improvements in how a person experiences a space.

Beyond that, TiD practitioners use the information they gained through the participatory design process to develop design solutions in which staff and clients feel safe and comfortable. This is done by learning about the community of users and developing an understanding of their lived experiences, to identify any stressors or potential triggers that might be present in the built environment, and then addressing those through the design.

In keeping with the SAMHSA guidance that trauma-informed approaches are "'hardwired' into practices" (SAMHSA, 2014), TiD practitioners should strive to mitigate identified issues with design elements rather than relying on behavior, memory, or training. For instance, if it is important to keep knives in a kitchen locked away, an feature that automatically locks the drawer when it is closed could be included rather than a manual lock.

The final essential feature of TiD in the built environment is ensuring that each key component of the 11 domains of the TiD Framework are tended to in the design. The following pages outline the key components of each domain, first introduced in the chapter on Trauma-informed Design, as well as the strategies necessary to meet them. Also included are tactics, which are examples of evidence that the key component is met.

KEY COMPONENTS

DOMAIN 1
Safety

Safety includes physical safety

Safety includes psychological safety

Safety is about how the individual feels

DOMAIN 2
Trustworthiness and Transparency

Transparency builds and maintains trust among staff, clients, and other interested parties.

DOMAIN 3
Peer Support

The inclusion of individuals with experiences of trauma supports understanding.

STRATEGIES

DOMAIN 4
Collaboration and Mutality

Building relationships that transcend organizational structure supports healing and enables collaboration.

DOMAIN 5
Empowerment and Voice

Recognizing and building upon individuals' strengths and experiences fosters empowerment.

Staff are provided organizational support and co-care.

KEY COMPONENTS

Clients are provided ample, meaningful choice and supported in decision-making and goal-setting.	**DOMAIN 6** **Choice**

Recognizing and addressing historical trauma supports the empowerment of all people.	Traditional cultural connections have healing value.	**DOMAIN 7** **Equity**

TACTICS

Incorporating and reflecting the community's culture promotes a sense of belonging.	**DOMAIN 8** **Community**

Ease, familiarity, and hominess contribute to comfort.	**DOMAIN 9** **Comfort**

Movement can help regulate the nervous system and enhance learning and healing processes.	**DOMAIN 10** **Movement**

Play is a building block in learning how to develop healthy relationships.	**DOMAIN 11** **Play**

DOMAIN ①

SAFETY

Aligns with the SAMHSA Principle of Safety: Throughout the organization, staff and the people they serve feel physically and psychologically safe.

Safety is the highest priority in implementing a trauma-informed approach. It applies to everyone, including staff, those receiving services, their support system, visitors, and children.

KEY COMPONENT A:
Safety includes physical safety.

The first key component of safety is often the most obvious: a person should be physically safe from injury, illness, and other dangers and hazards. This includes protection of their long-term health.

Physical Safety in Sphere I: Policy and Practice

The organization's policies and practices foster and protect the physical safety and long-term health of staff, clients, and other invested parties.

TID FRAMEWORK

Strategies

The physical environment, including staff areas, is well maintained and free from dangers and hazards to physical safety. An exception can be made for treatment, fitness, or adventure programs or activities, or for other organizations that operate primarily in natural settings, provided these programs obtain informed consent and adhere to safety best practices.

Staff are physically safe at work. Staff are not required to engage in dangerous activities, unless it is part of their job duties, they have given informed consent, they are specifically trained to do so, and the organization adheres to safety best practices.

Clients, visitors, and others are physically safe when interacting with the organization. The organization does not engage in practices that could physically harm clients, visitors, or others, nor does it:
* Contract or partner with organizations that engage in practices that could cause physical harm; or
* Require or coerce clients, visitors, or others to engage in practices that could cause themselves or others physical harm.

An exception can be made for disclosed risks of treatment, fitness, or adventure programs or activities, or for other organizations that operate primarily in natural settings, provided they obtain informed consent, and adhere to safety best practices.

The organization and all its staff interact in a trauma-informed way with one another, clients, visitors, and others. As experiencing high stress levels and re-traumatization can directly result in negative health outcomes, it is imperative that everyone at the organization understands and implements the key principles of trauma-informed care in all their interactions, to prevent harm.

Tactics

→ The organization complies with all federal, state, and local building, fire, accessibility, health, and occupational safety codes, standards, and regulations.

→ Staff have a clear understanding of their job duties and responsibilities, and receive proper and adequate training to carry them out.

→ The organization obtains informed consent prior to someone engaging in dangerous activities or environments.

→ The organization employs security or reception staff.

→ The organization has a means of monitoring who is present in its spaces and programs.

→ The organization uses security screenings for clients, visitors, or possibly staff. It is worth noting that, while this can contribute significantly to physical safety, it may negatively impact emotional safety. Security screenings, therefore, should only be used when the risk to physical safety cannot otherwise be sufficiently mitigated. This is often dependent upon the type of organization and the services it provides.

→ The organization ensures that all levels of staff receive on-going training and mentoring in trauma-informed care and approaches.

→ Staff members of all levels are evaluated on how well they implement trauma-informed care and approaches through regular performance reviews.

Physical Safety in Sphere II: Design Process

The design process is carried out in a way that fosters and protects the physical safety and long-term health of staff, clients, and all others involved.

Strategies

The physical environment in which the design team works is well maintained and free from dangers and hazards to physical safety. An exception can be made when operating in natural settings, provided they adhere to safety best practices.

The design team is physically safe at work. They are not required to engage in dangerous activities, unless it is part of their job duties, they have given informed consent, they are specifically trained to do so, and their firm adheres to safety best practices.

All clients and other participants are physically safe throughout the design process. The design team does not engage in practices that could physically harm clients or other participants, nor does it:

* Contract or partner with organizations that engage in practices that could cause physical harm; or
* Require or coerce clients or other participants to engage in practices that could cause themselves or others physical harm.

All members of the design team interact in a trauma-informed way with one another, clients, and others. As experiencing high stress levels and re-traumatization can directly result in negative health outcomes, it is imperative that everyone at the firm understands and implements the key principles of trauma-informed care in all their interactions, to prevent harm.

Tactics

→ The design firm complies with all federal, state, local building, fire, accessibility, health, and occupational safety codes, standards, and regulations.

→ The members of the design team have a clear understanding of their job duties and responsibilities, and receive proper and adequate training to carry them out.

→ The design firm obtains informed consent prior to a team member engaging in dangerous activities or environments.

→ The design firm employs security or reception staff.

→ The design firm has a means of monitoring who is present in its spaces and programs.

→ The design firm ensures that all design team members receive on-going training and mentoring in trauma-informed care and approaches.

TID FRAMEWORK

→ The design firm evaluates the performance of all design team members based on how well they implement trauma-informed care and approaches through regular performance reviews.

Physical Safety in Sphere III: Built Environment

The built environment fosters and protects the physical safety and long-term health of all who use the space.

Strategies

The built environment includes a variety of physical security features. This may include the use of automatically locking secure entries, cameras, or other hardening measures. It is worth noting that the use of some visible security hardening measures can affect users' sense of emotional safety. For this reason, TiD practitioners should discuss how clients and other invested parties feel about these measures and carefully weigh these feelings against the purpose of the project, to identify the benefits and drawbacks of their inclusion.

One type of security hardening of particular interest is security cameras, because if they are not constantly monitored, they have limited ability to prevent harm. Also, some users may feel surveilled in the environment if they are included. For this reason, it is important to discuss the possible inclusion of cameras with the community of users to ascertain their emotional response. If they would feel an added sense of safety from the presence of cameras, they may be worth including. If they have a negative reaction to security cameras, alternatives can include mirrors and motion lights.

The design minimizes the presence of physical hazards. When physical hazards do exist, the design includes features that minimize the risk of physical harm resulting.

Tactics

→ The design complies with all federal, state, local building, fire, accessibility, health, and occupational safety codes, standards, and regulations.

→ The design includes a variety of physical security features.

→ The design process included conversations with the client and other participants to elicit their feelings regarding physical security features, including security cameras and alternatives such as mirrors or motion lights.

→ The built environment includes emergency response equipment (e.g., defibrillators).

→ The built environment includes ligature-resistant hardware and furniture.

→ Emergency exit designs support all occupants, including those with disabilities.

→ The built environment includes fall- and slip-resistant designs (e.g., tall railings on elevated floorings to prevent jumping, anti-slip flooring).

→ There are no sharp edges on furniture or other surfaces.

→ All areas are well lit without producing glare.

→ Bathroom doors can be locked by users.

KEY COMPONENT B:
Safety includes psychological safety.

The TiD understanding of safety includes feeling psychologically safe about the interpersonal interactions taking place.

Psychological Safety in Sphere I: Policy and Practice

The organization's policies and practices foster and protect the psychological safety of staff, clients, and other invested parties.

Strategies

Clients, visitors, and others feel safe when interacting with the organization. The organization does not coerce or force them to do anything they perceive as harmful, nor does it cause emotional or psychological harm to clients or others.

Staff feel safe at work. Staff are not required to do anything they perceive as harmful. The organization does not tolerate harassment, bullying, or other hostile environments.

The organization offers trainings and has a written policy on harassment. The training is mandatory for staff and optional for others, and covers what harassment is, how to report it, and what supports are available for staff and others who do not feel safe. The policy includes a clear procedure through which grievances or allegations of harassment can been made and will be reviewed. The organization invites input from staff, clients, and other invested parties when revising its policies.

The organization provides supports for individuals who report not feeling safe. These may include one-on-one support, the development of a safety plan, and peer support opportunities.

The organization actively gathers input from staff, clients, and others on its practices, and uses that feedback to refine operations.

Clients and staff feel capable and confident to be their authentic selves when interacting with the organization.

Tactics

➜ Staff have written documentation that clearly outlines their job duties and expectations.

➜ The organization has open discussions with, and provides written information, clients and others regarding its practices.

➜ The organization regularly surveys clients and staff regarding their sense of safety.

→ The organization has written policies and procedures.

→ The organization regularly reviews and updates its policies and practices based on feedback received.

→ The organization has a policy that outlines how to respond in an emergency or crisis.

→ The organization has a policy that outlines its approach to handling harassing, bullying, and other hostile behavior.

→ The organization has an anti-discrimination policy and expectations.

→ The organization provides regular training or professional development opportunities for staff on topics of justice, equity, diversity and inclusion (JEDI).

→ The organization engages with clients and others on JEDI topics and in community or cultural events.

→ Staff regularly check-in with clients about how they are doing and if there is anything they can do to make them feel more comfortable or safe.

→ The organization engages in debriefing practices, which involve clients and all levels of staff, following significant, dangerous, or traumatic events, and uses the information learned to inform changes to practice and policy to protect against recurrence.

Psychological Safety in Sphere II: Design Process

The design process is carried out in a way that fosters and protects the psychological safety of staff, clients, and all others involved.

Strategies

All clients and other participants feel safe throughout the design process.
The design team is transparent about its processes, expectations, timelines, limitations, and deliverables. They use inclusive, trauma-informed language, and ensure the process is as welcoming and comfortable as possible. The team is prepared for personal disclosures and does not press difficult topics when they are not directly relevant to the project. They are able to recognize when a participant becomes dysregulated and provide appropriate support. Participants feel respected and heard.

Design team staff feel safe throughout the design process. Staff are equipped to engage clients and other participants in a trauma-informed process and to support dysregulated participants. All members of the design team recognize that mistakes will happen, and when they do, they respond appropriately by making one another aware, apologizing, and taking care not to repeat the mistake in the future. To ward off vicarious trauma, team members support one another and the firm actively provides and engages in stress-relieving measures.

The design firm offers mandatory staff trainings and has a written policy on harassment. The training covers what harassment is, how to report it, and what supports are available for anyone who does not feel safe. The policy includes a clear procedure through which grievances or allegations of harassment can been made and will be reviewed. The design firm invites input from staff, clients, and other invested parties when revising its policies.

The design firm provides supports for individuals who report not feeling safe. These may include one-on-one support, the development of a safety plan, and peer support opportunities.

The design team actively gathers input from clients and other participants on its design process, and uses that feedback to refine future events.

Tactics

➜ Participants receive reliable communication and scheduling throughout the process.

→ Participatory design activities are well-planned and run on schedule.

→ Facilitators are assisted by other practitioners who can provide support to participants who struggle or become dysregulated.

→ Facilitators do not push for details about topics not directly related to the project.

→ Participants are informed if, and why, any of their recommendations were not included in the final design.

→ The design team uses trauma-informed, inclusive language.

→ The design team uses trauma-informed interview practices.

→ Any written materials for the project use trauma-informed, inclusive language.

→ The design firm provides project-specific training on impacts affecting the intended users of the space (e.g., information about the neighborhood, population of users, social determinants of health).

→ The design team is aware of the culture of participants and the intended community of users, and dress and interact (including in their body language) in a way that is respectful of that culture.

→ Members of the design team provide co-care for one another by sharing work, encouraging self-care, reaching out to struggling coworkers personally, and encouraging struggling team members to seek employee assistance or mental health services.

→ Staff are encouraged by supervisors and the firm to engage in self-care, including time away from the job, and are not judged or penalized in any way for doing so.

→ The firm provides co-care for staff by allowing them to disconnect completely, offering trainings on resiliency, and providing fitness center memberships, wellness programs, assistance programs, and mental health services.

TID FRAMEWORK

→ The design team surveys participants, or holds focus groups, to gather input on the process and makes refinements based on the feedback received.

Psychological Safety in Sphere III: Built Environment

The built environment fosters and protects the psychological safety of all who use the space.

Strategies

Clients, visitors, and others feel safe in the space. They feel safe when entering the building. Once inside, their senses are not overwhelmed and they can maneuver and find their way around easily. There are no spaces in which they feel trapped or cornered. They believe their private details are well-protected. If they become dysregulated, they know there is a space where they can try to regulate their systems.

Staff feel safe and are able to regulate their emotions while at work. They can see who is nearby or coming in their direction. They know that their private information is well-protected.

Members of the Lesbian, Gay, Bisexual, Transgender, Queer/Questioning, Intersex, Asexual, Plus (LGBTQIA+) community feel safe in the space.

Biophilic patterns that can lower blood pressure and increase the perception of safety are included in the design. These include visual, non-visual, and material connection to nature, prospect, and refuge.
Clients, visitors, staff, and others feel welcome and that they belong in the space.

Tactics

→ Gathering spaces, including smoking areas, are not located directly outside the building's entrances.

→ There is adequate lighting in parking areas, along walkways, and throughout the space.

→ Noise levels are tolerable and not overwhelming.

→ There are places where private or confidential conversations can be had without fear that they can be overheard.

→ There are no overpowering odors in the space.

→ Hallways and walkways are free from obstacles.

→ The space complies with accessibility standards.

→ There is clear wayfinding throughout the space.

→ There are clear sightlines throughout the space, into rooms, and through doors.

→ There are security measures to protect private information, such as locking filing cabinets, security screens on computer monitors, sound-proofing or -mitigating features in areas where private conversations occur, and curtains or blinds on windows.

→ There are clearly identifiable areas for use by clients, visitors, or others who are trying to regulate.

→ There are a variety of regulation spaces to accommodate a range of stress responses. These may include spaces in which individuals can expend physical energy through movement, reduce stimulus exposure, or gradually re-engage with environmental stimuli.

→ The space includes staff-only spaces, designed to help staff regulate their systems.

→ There are gender-neutral bathrooms for use by clients, visitors, or others.

→ There are gender-neutral bathrooms for staff.

→ Bathrooms are either single units or closet-style, with floor-to-ceiling partitions.

→ There are private, locked spaces where staff, clients, visitors, and others can store their belongings.

→ There are options for end-users to adapt their environment to their preferences, such as lighting controls, thermostats, and window coverings.

→ There are visual, non-visual, and material connections with nature within, or accessible from, the built environment.

→ There are areas in the built environment where a person can view who is present and what is happening from a distance.

→ There are areas in the built environment where a person can withdraw from the main happenings in the space, while being shielded from behind and overhead.

→ The artwork, colors, and symbols used throughout the space represent the cultures of its users, including clients, visitors, and staff.

KEY COMPONENT C:
Safety is about how the individual feels.

TiD practitioners recognize that there is no objective measure of a person's sense of safety. It is not enough that, based on logical consideration of the facts, a reasonable person would deem the individual safe from physical and emotional harm. The individual, themself, must feel safe in the environment and with the interactions taking place. If the person does not feel safe, their stress levels can be impacted regardless of what others think of the situation. Therefore, any concerns the individual has need to be taken seriously and addressed.

Individual Sense of Safety in Sphere I: Policy and Practice

The organization's policies and practices foster positive interactions and are responsive to the needs of clients, visitors, staff, and others.

98

Strategies

Clients, visitors, and others feel safe when interacting with the organization. They perceive their interactions within the organization to be positive, and believe that the organization is responsive to their needs and concerns.

Staff feel safe at work. They believe they can raise concerns without negative repercussions. They feel safe to innovate and take calculated risks in their work, and know that if something does not go well, their supervisors and management will support them, as needed, to problem-solve or address the concern.

The organization provides supports for individuals who report not feeling safe. These may include one-on-one support, the development of a safety plan, and peer support opportunities.

The organization actively gathers input from staff, clients, visitors, and others, and uses that feedback to address any personal concerns as quickly as possible.

Clients and staff feel capable and confident to be their authentic selves when interacting with the organization.

Tactics

→ Clients, visitors, and others report feeling safe when interacting with the organization.

→ Clients, visitors, and others regularly and openly discuss their safety concerns with staff.

→ Staff report feeling safe at work.

→ Staff ask clients what they can do to make them feel more safe.

→ Staff are empowered to, and skilled at, adapting their approach to address personal safety concerns raised by staff, clients, visitors, and others.

→ Staff who make mistakes or find themselves in difficult situations are supported in addressing the situation.

→ Staff who raise concerns do not face negative repercussions.

Individual Sense of Safety in Sphere II: Design Process

The design process is carried out in a way that fosters positive interactions and is responsive to the needs of clients, visitors, staff , and others.

Strategies

All clients and other participants feel safe throughout the design process. If they become dysregulated, they receive adequate support from the design team. They perceive the process as a positive experience, and believe that the design team is responsive to their needs and concerns.

Design team members feel safe throughout the design process. They believe they can raise concerns without negative repercussions. They feel prepared to safely lead participatory design processes, and know that if something does not go well, their team and firm will support them in working with dysregulated participants and addressing concerns.

The design firm provides supports for individuals who report not feeling safe. These may include one-on-one support, the development of a safety plan, and peer support opportunities.

The design team actively gathers input from clients and other participants, and uses that feedback to address any personal concerns as quickly as possible. Clients and staff feel capable and confident to be their authentic selves throughout the design process.

Tactics

→ Participants report feeling safe throughout the design process.

→ Participants openly discuss their safety concerns with the design team.

→ Design team members report feeling safe and prepared throughout the design process.

→ The design team asks participants what they can do to make them feel more safe.

→ Design team members are empowered to, and skilled at, adapting their approach to address personal safety concerns raised by participants.

→ Design team members are actively supported by the team and firm in addressing safety concerns.

→ Staff who raise concerns do not face negative repercussions.

Individual Sense of Safety in Sphere III: Built Environment

The built environment includes spaces that foster positive interactions and a sense of safety.

Strategies

Clients, visitors, and staff feel there are places within the built environment that allow for positive interactions. This can include a myriad of things, including spaces to congregate, talk privately or in groups, share food, engage in play, sit silently together, watch movies, listen to music, workout, or help one another regulate.

TID FRAMEWORK

Clients, visitors, and staff feel there are places for them to retreat. This can be in the form of nooks, small regulation spaces, or spaces that provide the sense of refuge within larger spaces.

The biophilic patterns of prospect and refuge, which can lower stress levels and increase the perception of safety, are included in the design. The goal is to provide staff, clients, visitors, and others with places in which they can retreat and surveille activity in the space.

Staff feel as though there are places for them to engage in positive interactions with others. This can include spaces just for staff, as well as places where staff and clients, visitors, and others can engage together.

Tactics

→ There are multiple gathering spaces of different types throughout the space, including offices, conference rooms, and other spaces that allow for a variety of types of activities and interactions.

→ There are a variety of seating options available in gathering spaces.

→ There are gathering spaces and places of retreat.

→ Gathering spaces and places of retreat are accessible.

→ There are staff-only break or regulation areas.

→ There are areas in the built environment where a person can withdraw from the main happenings in the space, while being shielded from behind and overhead.

→ There are areas in the built environment where a person can view who is present and what is happening from a distance.

→ There are private spaces for staff and clients to discuss private or confidential issues, which include features that prevent others outside the space from overhearing conversations (e.g., sound-proofing or -mitigating features) or seeing into the space (e.g., solid walls, curtains, blinds).

→ There are staff-only places in the built-environment that allow for both retreat and engagement.

→ Windows into spaces can have their transparency adjusted, or be covered or obscured, by users, allowing them to control their visibility to those outside the space.

TID FRAMEWORK

DOMAIN

TRUSTWORTHINESS AND TRANSPARENCY

Aligns with the SAMHSA Principle of Trustworthiness and Transparency: Operations and decisions are conducted with transparency with the goal of building and maintaining trust.

Trustworthiness and transparency is crucial to developing strong relationships with staff, clients, and others. In strong relationships we feel safe, can seek and offer support, and buffer one another's stress levels.

Predictability allows individuals to start to feel safe from unexpected, unpleasant surprises or circumstances. This is not to say that all encounters will be pleasant, but that the trust that has developed between the parties allows them to engage in difficult situations and conversations with a sense of safety and fairness.

KEY COMPONENT: Transparency builds and maintains trust among staff, clients, and other invested parties.

Transparency helps build trust in relationships. When a person knows what to expect from another, they can begin to develop a belief in the reliability and truth of their words and expressed principles. As each follows through on their words consistently over time, they can become more secure in the reliability of their actions. These are the foundations of trust.

As this is about forging strong, healthy relationships throughout the organization and all those it serves, transparency should extend to staff, clients, family members, volunteers, and others involved in the organization.

Building and Maintaining Trust in Sphere I: Policy and Practice

The organization's policies and practices require transparency and foster the development of enduring trust.

Strategies

The organization has written policies, and makes them available to staff, clients, and other invested parties. These policies include a clear procedure through which grievances can be made and for the review of any allegations of ethical or other violations, including inappropriate contacts, the sharing of private or confidential information, violent or dangerous behavior, sexual or other harassment, and discrimination. The organization invites input from staff, clients, and other invested parties when revising its policies.

The organization's practices align with its written policies. The organization regularly encourages behaviors that embody their policies and condemns behaviors that are in contrast to their policies. When grievances have been filed, they are promptly reviewed and addressed. The organization reprimands those who have committed a violation, in a consistent and equitable manner that does not demonstrate favoritism or discrimination.

The organization maintains the privacy and confidentiality of client information and informs clients about the extent and limits of these protections. Clients should understand: what staff are required to keep confidential; what they are required to disclose, to whom, and in what timeframes; and what they may share with staff or others involved in the client's case or services.

Clients are informed about the organization's services. This includes not only what services are available and their associated costs, but also what each entails and how, when, and by whom they will be provided. The client is informed about

TID FRAMEWORK

any rights they may have throughout their interactions with the organization. If the organization has expectations of clients, these are also shared.

Staff demonstrate they value clients by engaging with respect, compassion, and collaboration. Clients recognize that staff are committed to building long-term relationships.

There is consistency in responses to staff, clients, and others throughout the organization. Staff are supported in developing this consistency through structures such as: the sharing of policies, practices, and program information; trainings and professional development; meetings; and supportive supervision. Staff are held accountable for complying with the organization's policies and practices.

Staff are reliable. They follow-through on commitments and keep scheduled appointments and meetings. If there is a necessary cancellation, they notify others as soon as possible and reschedule.

Tactics

→ The organization shares its written policies with the public on a regular basis or upon request, including the grievance and allegation review procedures.

→ Staff members of all levels are evaluated on how well they comply with the organization's policies and practices through regular performance reviews.

→ Clients are provided with information about services and their rights and responsibilities, in a language they can understand.

→ Clients understand what and how the organization collects, protects, uses, shares, and destroys their private, personal, and protected information, as well as how the information they can access or share it.

→ Rules or community agreements are posted by the organization.

→ The organization uses translation and interpretation services to ensure accessibility for those who may have language access needs.

➜ Staff do not talk about clients in public spaces or with anyone not involved in the client's case or services.

➜ Staff treat clients with respect and compassion.

➜ Staff follow-through on commitments and keep scheduled appointments and meetings.

➜ Records that are no longer required are securely destroyed.

Building and Maintaining Trust in Sphere II: Design Process
The design process requires transparency and fosters trust.

Strategies

Participants are informed about the design process. This includes the goals of the project, reason for seeking feedback, limitations, what the participant's commitment or involvement entails, and scheduling details. Participants are also made aware of potential risks or discomfort they may encounter through their participation. Plain language is used, and translation or interpretation services are made available to participants. Participants are given the opportunity to ask questions or seek clarification before committing to their participation.

Interactive design sessions and passive user-input activities are well thought-out and structured. This indicates to participants that the design team values and respects their time. Translations and interpreters are used when necessary. The session or activity affords enough time for participants to share the context behind their feedback, which is accurately recorded by the design team.

Participants are informed about what information will be collected and how it will be stored and used. Prior to engaging in the design process, the design team informs participants what specific data will be collected through each activity, including through digital, hand-written, audio- or video-recorded, and prototyped or created mediums. Staff details how all data will be collected, transcribed, analyzed, stored, and shared including: format; storage location; parties who will have access and whether it will be anonymized; how long it will be stored; measures taken to restrict and control access (e.g., encryption); and any intent to aggregate and analyze data for purposes of the project, publication, presentation, or future analysis.

The design team members are reliable. They follow-through on commitments and keep scheduled appointments and meetings. If there is a necessary cancellation, they notify others as soon as possible and reschedule.

The design team follows up with participants. In the short term, this includes providing key written take-aways from the session. Once the initial design is completed, the design team presents it to participants and, if any feedback was not able to be incorporated, addresses the reasons. Participants are offered another opportunity to provide feedback, which the design team uses to refine the design.

Tactics

➜ The design provides participants with comprehensive details about the design process in a format they can understand and provides participants the opportunity to opt in or out.

➜ The design team provides participants with written notes that summarize the session and its outcomes.

➜ The design team follows-through on commitments and keeps scheduled appointments and meetings.

➜ Interpreters are scheduled, when necessary, for participatory design sessions.

➜ The design team explains their decisions regarding the inclusion of feedback to participants.

➜ The design process is iterative and provides multiple opportunities for feedback from participants.

Building and Maintaining Trust in Sphere III: Built Environment

The built environment requires transparency and fosters the development of enduring trust.

Strategies

Staff and clients are assured that their personal and confidential information is protected. This includes information that is shared in a written or verbal form.

Tactics

→ There are private spaces for staff and clients to discuss private or confidential issues, which include features that prevent others outside the space from overhearing conversations (e.g., sound-proofing or -mitigating features) or seeing into the space (e.g., solid walls, curtains, blinds).

→ There is locked storage for personal and confidential information.

→ There are security features on hardware and software systems that prevent the inadvertent sharing of information (e.g., password protection, firewalls, security screens).

→ There is information available in the built environment about the current air quality.

→ There is a mechanism by which users can identify where the materials used in the built environment were sourced or the supplier company's practices (e.g., bar codes, QR codes).

→ There is information available to users about the products and methods used to maintain the space (e.g., cleaners, chemicals, methods that would affect air quality or individuals with sensitivities).

TID FRAMEWORK

→ There is signage in the built environment that informs users how they can contact the facility's management team.

→ Community agreements are easily viewable in the built environment.

→ There are operable windows with the ability for users to cover them or adjust their transparency, to both outside and inside spaces, throughout the built environment.

→ Wayfinding that is prominent, supportive, and shown in different mediums to ensure comprehension by a range of cognitive, physical, and cultural identities.

→ The built environment includes readily visible and available options for accessibility (e.g., ramps, call buttons, places to rest on pathways).

→ There are places throughout the built environment for users to provide suggestions regarding improvements to policy, practice, and environment.

Trustworthiness and Transparency

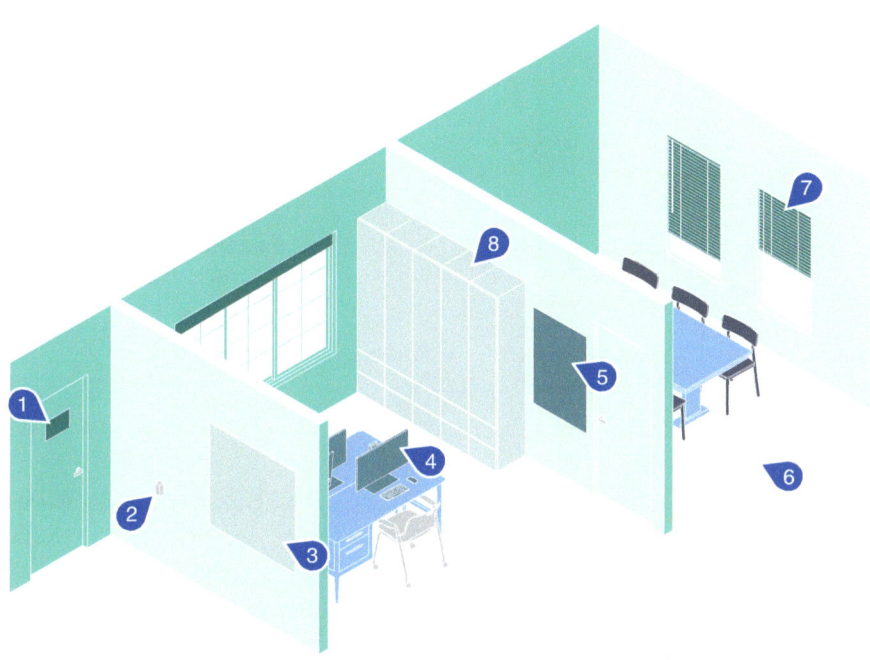

1. Wayfinding signage
2. Door opener
3. Daily activity board
4. Digital privacy and security

5. Community agreement
6. Acoustically private room
7. Windows with blinds
8. Secure storage

Illustration by Architecture for Public Benefit

Figure 10. Trustworthiness and Transparency in the built environment

TID FRAMEWORK

DOMAIN ③

PEER SUPPORT

Aligns with the SAMHSA Principle of Peer Support: Peer support and mutual self-help are key vehicles for establishing safety and hope, building trust, enhancing collaboration, and utilizing stories and experiences to promote recovery and healing.

To be trauma-informed, we need to recognize, respect, and honor the fact that we are all multicultural beings, composed of multiple social and cultural identities. These identities inform the way we interpret and understand our experiences. In a sense, they make up who we are, while also shaping how we see the world around us and how we fit into it.

This necessitates that we also recognize that every individual interprets the world through their own, individual lens. In short, it is impossible to ever fully understand how another person experiences things. Unless we live through every single experience of their lives, in the same environment, with the same supports and people—and even the same genetic make-up—we can never truly understand how they might experience or be impacted by a situation. Furthermore, the perspective of one person does not, and cannot, represent the views of all people with similar experiences, or who share similar identities.

This creates a conundrum for the TiD practitioner, as the key method is to use information gathered from research, focus groups, and interviews to identify design features intended to mitigate stressors in the built environment. In our quest to achieve this task, we look to SAMHSA's guidance for a way forward.

When developing the key principles, SAMHSA included peer support, in "recognition that those similar experiences can more deeply understand and relate to a person's experience" (SAMHSA, 2014). So, even though we may never be able to fully understand how any individual may react to a situation or environment, gathering information and feedback from a variety of individuals with similar backgrounds and experiences can help us develop a better composite from which to work.

SAMHSA also noted that having one's experience validated by others fosters a sense of belonging. This is key, as survivors often feel distanced from family and friends, who have difficulty understanding their reactions. As traumas frequently erode survivors' ability to trust, a principle element of peer support is the development, or rebuilding, of pro-social skills and interactions.

It is for these reasons that the inclusion of peers in all three spheres of TiD is so important.

KEY COMPONENT:
Peer groups support understanding and a sense of belonging.

Individuals who experienced similar traumatic experiences as, and who share similar identities and other life experiences with, the clients being served by an organization, or in a specific space, can provide the most accurate and useful feedback to inform policies, practices, design processes, and the ultimate design. Peer groups also foster a sense of belonging among survivors. Peer support opportunities can be formal (e.g., regularly scheduled groups) or informal (e.g., individuals gathering to enjoy an activity together or support someone in need).

Inclusion of Peer Support in Sphere I: Policy and Practice

Individuals who experienced similar traumatic experiences as, and share similar identities and other life experiences with, the organization's clients are involved in developing its policies and practices. The organization's policies and practices encourage engagement in peer support.

TID FRAMEWORK

Strategies

There are opportunities for clients to engage in peer support groups or activities. The organization encourages such participation in various ways, such as by supporting the groups financially, offsetting participation costs, making referrals, and offering childcare for parents while they participate. Peer support opportunities are also offered and encouraged for children.

There are opportunities for staff to engage in peer support groups or activities. The organization encourages such participation in similar ways, and may also allow participation during regularly scheduled work hours.

The organization actively recruits individuals with lived experience to serve as employees and in advisory roles.

The organization implements strategies to encourage staff to use, and refer others to, peer support opportunities.

Tactics

→   Formal peer support groups exist.

→   Staff engage in social activities outside of work hours and functions.

→   Staff makes referrals to peer support programs on a regular basis.

→   Former clients are employed by the organization, or serve in an advisory capacity or on its board.

→   The organization solicits feedback from children and youth in an age-appropriate manner.

Inclusion of Peer Support in Sphere II: Design Process

Individuals who experienced similar traumatic experiences as, and share similar identities and other life experiences with, the organization's clients are involved in the design process. The design firm encourages engagement in peer support.

Strategies

The design team is proficient at facilitating, and regularly engages in, participatory design processes.

Knowing that individuals with past traumatic experiences will be participating in design sessions, the design team engages with these individuals in trauma-informed ways such as using appropriate language and providing supporting resources. Team members are equipped to engage clients and other participants in a trauma-informed process and to support dysregulated participants.

Design team members provide one another with co-care, to support one another and protect against vicarious trauma.

Tactics

➔ The final design includes features developed as a result of feedback received from individuals with lived experience.

➔ Participants with lived experience stay engaged throughout the process.

➔ Participants with lived experience validate one another's experiences and feedback.

➔ Design team members support one another in responding to anyone who becomes dysregulated.

➔ Design team members encourage one another, and refer one another to formal peer support services when appropriate.

TID FRAMEWORK

Inclusion of Peer Support in Sphere III: Built Environment

The built environment fosters the inclusion of peer support throughout the organization's operations.

Strategies

There are meeting spaces that can accommodate members of the public and individuals with lived experience. These spaces should be accessible to individuals of all abilities.

The built environment includes spaces designed to foster prosocial interactions among staff, clients, visitors, and others. These should be varied and/or adaptable, to allow for as many types of interactions as possible.

Tactics

➔ There are a variety of types and sizes of gathering spaces, including outdoor options.

➔ There are staff-only spaces.

➔ There are spaces for peer groups to meet.

➔ There are places that encourage participation of larger groups.

➔ There are various types and arrangements of seating, so users can sit with as many, or as few, other people as feels safe. These seating options also allow users to choose the angle at which they face, or do not face, others.

➔ Seating options and room configuration and size allow for more formal meetings, as well as more relaxed social interactions.

➔ If the space includes a secure perimeter, there are meeting spaces outside the highest-security areas.

Peer Support

1.	Accessible entry		**4.**	Large flexible space
2.	Outdoor seating options		**5.**	Collaborative space
3.	Modular configurable furniture		**6.**	Private comfortable area

Illustration by Architecture for Public Benefit

Figure 11. Peer Support in the built environment

DOMAIN ④

COLLABORATION AND MUTUALITY

Aligns with the SAMHSA Principle of Collaboration and Mutuality: Everyone has a role to play in a trauma-informed approach, regardless of their role in the organization.

Healing happens in relationships and the meaningful sharing of power and decision making. Collaboration and mutuality focuses on the importance of partnering with everyone and leveling the power differences between staff, clients, and others, throughout the organization. This makes room for diverse viewpoints, which is vital due to our limited ability to share other's perspectives (see the Peer Support section for more information), and leads to better outcomes.

By incorporating a wider group into decision-making, we can increase transparency, empowerment, voice, and choice. The goal is to build relationships that transcend structure, so everyone can work together towards a common objective. As power dynamics exist in nearly every group, it may not be possible to completely eliminate the hierarchy, but efforts should be made to flatten the structure as much as possible and encourage conversations and information sharing across the strata.

KEY COMPONENT:
Building relationships that transcend organizational structure supports healing and enables collaboration.

In trauma-informed organizations, everyone has a role in supporting others, regardless of their position. Sometimes relationships are forged between the most unlikeliest of people. As we cannot predict who will form a relationship that helps someone build resilience, everyone should be encouraged to engage across the organization. In such an environment, relationships can flourish and staff, clients, and others can all work together towards a common goal.

Fostering Cross-Sectional Relationships in Sphere I: Policy and Practice

The organization's policies and practices support collaboration with, and foster relationship-building among, staff of all levels, clients, and others.

Strategies

The organization fosters relationships between staff, clients, and others. This can include hosting events through which they can get to know one another personally and allowing time in meetings for participants to connect authentically.

The organization invites input from staff, clients, and other invested parties. Such feedback is solicited regularly, both with regard to the provision of services and when conducting policy reviews. The organization uses the feedback received to inform the revision of its policies and practices. Staff address any concerns raised, and change their approach in response to feedback, when appropriate.

Tactics

→ Relationships exist among staff across various roles and levels of organizational structure.

TID FRAMEWORK

→ The organization regularly incorporates feedback from staff across tenure, responsibilities, and roles.

→ The organization solicits feedback from clients and other invested parties.

→ The organization includes some of its former clients as employees, in an advisory capacity, or on its board.

→ Children and youth are given systematic opportunities to voice needs and concerns in an age-appropriate manner.

→ Staff have regular meetings with organizational management and leadership.

→ The organization engages external partners.

Fostering Cross-Sectional Relationships in Sphere II: Design Process

The design firm supports collaboration with participants and fosters relationship-building among staff of all levels.

Strategies

The design firm fosters relationships among staff of all levels. This can include hosting events through which they can get to know one another personally and allowing time in meetings for participants to connect authentically.

The design team regularly engages in participatory design processes to solicit feedback from staff, clients, and other invested parties. When relevant to the project, this includes involving children and youth.

Tactics

→ Relationships exist among staff across various roles and levels of the firm's organizational structure.

→ The design team meets regularly with firm management and leadership.

→ The design team regularly solicits feedback from clients and other invested parties to inform the design and its processes.

→ The final design includes features developed as a result of feedback received from individuals with lived experience.

→ Individuals of diverse backgrounds and roles regularly participate in the design process.

→ Collaborative activities are included throughout the design process rather than in isolation.

→ Participants of collaborative activities are informed of any instances where their feedback or input was not included, and why.

Fostering Cross-Sectional Relationships in Sphere III: Built Environment

The built environment supports collaboration with, and fosters relationship-building among, staff of all levels, clients, and others.

Strategies

There are meeting spaces that can accommodate members of the public and individuals with lived experience. These spaces should be accessible to individuals of all abilities.

The built environment includes spaces designed to support collaboration.
These should be varied and/or adaptable, to allow for as many types of interactions as possible.

Tactics

→   There are a variety of types and sizes of gathering spaces that support both formal (e.g., meeting, professional development, structured activity) and informal interactions.

→   There are places that encourage participation of larger groups.

→   The spaces include adjustable, ergonomic seating to maximize user comfort.

→   If the space includes a secure perimeter, there are meeting spaces outside the highest-security areas to allow members of the public to participate in meetings without having to clear a security check-point.

DOMAIN ⑤

EMPOWERMENT AND VOICE

Aligns with the SAMHSA Principle of Empowerment, Voice, and Choice: Staff are the facilitators of recovery, and may experience various levels of trauma themselves.

A trauma-informed approach fosters empowerment for staff and clients alike. While this is similar to collaboration and mutuality, empowerment focuses specifically on the services provided to a client, or the support provided to a staff member, and their level of participation and control throughout.

KEY COMPONENT A:
Recognizing and building upon individuals' strengths and experiences fosters empowerment.

Empowerment is fostered through a belief in the primacy of the people served, resilience, and the ability to heal and promote recovery from trauma. Clients are supported in cultivating self-advocacy skills.

Leveraging Individual Strengths in Sphere I:
Policy and Practice

The organization's policies and practices build upon clients' strengths and expe-riences, provides them some control in the provision of services, and aids them in developing resiliency and self-advocacy skills.

Strategies

The organization recognizes that clients can provide invaluable information regarding their own care, and supports and engages them in decision-making and the planning of services. Service plans are individualized and created with the client's input. Clients are fully involved in decisions related to service planning, information sharing, and progress monitoring. Service plans are designed to ensure that clients identify their personal strengths and goals.

Clients are aware of, and understand, the services and resources available to them. Staff help clients explore the options and identify which are best suited for them, based on their specific circumstances.

Clients are supported in developing resiliency and self-advocacy skills. The organization provides educational opportunities for clients on the impacts of stress and traumatic experiences and strengthening resiliency.

Clients have a way to monitor their progress and the effectiveness of services on a routine basis.

Tactics

→ Clients feel as though they have control in decision-making and the planning of services.

→ Clients feel comfortable inviting personal supports to planning meetings.

→ Children and youth are given systematic, age-appropriate opportunities to voice needs, concerns, and experiences.

TID FRAMEWORK

➔ The organization engages in person-centered planning, in which the individual receiving services provides the information on which their service plan is based.

➔ Service plans include the client's strengths and goals, as identified by both staff and the client.

➔ Staff provide clients with information about available services and resources.

➔ Clients are aware of ways to manage stress and build resiliency.

➔ Staff obtain informed consent from clients prior to, and throughout, the provision of services.

Leveraging Individual Strengths in Sphere II: Design Process

The design process builds upon participants' strengths and experiences, provides them some control over the process, and aids clients in self-advocacy.

Strategies

The design team recognizes that clients can provide invaluable information regarding the environment in which services are provided, and engages in trauma-informed participatory processes to encourage the sharing of insights and feedback. Participants are encouraged to participate and advocate for themselves throughout the design process. The design team creates a diverse, inclusive, equitable, and safe space for collaboration and co-design.

Participatory and collaborative activities leverage various ways of providing input. Participants are not just invited to participate but enabled to participate according to their abilities and preferences. The design team provides accommodations for those with disabilities, as well as opportunities to provide input in multiple formats, such as: written and visual; live and asynchronous; and individually and as a team.

TID FRAMEWORK

Tactics

➔ The design team tells participants their experiences afford them a unique perspective, vital in creating a service delivery space that optimizes the client experience.

➔ The design team responds to feedback from participants regarding the design process itself, and makes changes to accommodate the safety and comfort of participants.

➔ The design process is iterative and provides multiple opportunities for feed-back from participants.

➔ The design team explains their decisions regarding the inclusion of feedback to participants. Participants are informed if, and why, any of their recommendations were not included in the final design.

➔ The design team uses the predominate language of the community and uses translation and interpretation services to ensure accessibility for those who may have language access needs.

➔ The design team uses trauma-informed, inclusive language (see Appendix A).

➔ The design team uses language that is easily understood by the community and avoids industry-specific language and jargon.

➔ The design team uses trauma-informed interview practices.

➔ The design team recognizes and mitigates potential hierarchies, tensions, or cultural norms that may impact interactions (e.g., using a local facilitator or moderator).

➔ Any written materials for the project use trauma-informed, inclusive language.

Leveraging Individual Strengths in Sphere III: Built Environment

The built environment encourages the empowerment of clients and supports the development of resilience and self-advocacy skills.

Strategies

The built environment includes spaces where staff and clients can engage together in decision making and planning.

The built environment includes spaces in which the organization can conduct or facilitate trainings and educational opportunities for clients. These spaces should be able to accommodate classes supported by audio-visual and reading materials, as well as more active classes designed to build stress-management skills (e.g., yoga, fitness).

Tactics

→ There are a variety of types and sizes of gathering spaces.

→ Meeting spaces include adjustable, ergonomic seating, to maximize user comfort.

→ Seating options and room configuration and size allow for more formal meetings and classes as well as activities with less restricted movement.

→ There are a variety of places for people to gather or engage in self-care, including outdoor options.

KEY COMPONENT B:
Staff are provided organizational support and co-care.

In this model, there is an understanding that anyone may have experienced trauma,

TID FRAMEWORK

including those running the organization or providing services. Staff receive organizational support, which enables them to become highly proficient at their jobs.

Staff Support in Sphere I: Policy and Practice

The organization's policies and practices support staff and ensure the provision of co-care.

Strategies

Staff are supported in recognizing and addressing their responses to stress.
The organization provides regular training or professional development opportunities for staff on vicarious trauma and how to manage their stress levels and mitigate any potential impacts. The organization has a system in place to evaluate the social and emotional experience of staff and ensure debriefing practices after significant, dangerous, or traumatic events.

Tactics

→ Staff provide co-care for one another by sharing work, encouraging self-care, reaching out to struggling coworkers, and encouraging struggling team members to seek employee assistance or mental health services.

→ Staff are encouraged by supervisors and the firm to engage in self-care, including time away from the job, and are not judged or penalized in any way for doing so.

→ The organization provides co-care for staff by allowing them to disconnect completely, offering trainings on resiliency, and providing fitness center memberships, wellness programs, assistance programs, and mental health services.

Staff Support in Sphere II: Design Process

The design process supports the design team and ensures the provision of co-care.

Strategies

Design team members are supported in recognizing and addressing their responses to stress. The firm provides regular training or professional development opportunities for staff on vicarious trauma and how to manage their stress levels and mitigate any potential impacts. The firm has a system in place to evaluate the social and emotional experience of staff and ensure debriefing practices after significant, dangerous, or traumatic events.

Tactics

→ Members of the design team provide co-care for one another by sharing work, encouraging self-care, reaching out to struggling coworkers personally, and encouraging struggling team members to seek employee assistance or mental health services.

→ Staff are encouraged by supervisors and the firm to engage in self-care, including time away from the job, and are not judged or penalized in any way for doing so.

→ The firm provides co-care for design team members by allowing them to disconnect completely, offering trainings on resiliency, and providing fitness center memberships, wellness programs, assistance programs, and mental health services.

→ The design team surveys participants or holds focus groups to gather input on the process and makes refinements based on the feedback received.

TID FRAMEWORK

Staff Support in Sphere III: Built Environment

The built environment includes spaces in which staff can receive support and co-care.

Strategies

The built environment includes spaces in which the organization can conduct or facilitate trainings and professional development opportunities for clients. These spaces should be able to accommodate classes supported by audio-visual and reading materials, as well as more active classes designed to build stress-management skills (e.g., yoga, fitness).

The built environment includes spaces in which staff can regulate their emotions.

Tactics

➜   There are staff-only break or regulation areas.

➜   There are a variety of types and sizes of gathering spaces, including outdoor options.

➜   Meeting spaces include adjustable, ergonomic seating, to maximize user comfort.

➜   Seating options and room configuration and size allow for more formal meetings and classes as well as activities with less restricted movement.

➜   There are a variety of places outside for people to regulate, including outdoor options.

TID FRAMEWORK

DOMAIN ⑥

CHOICE

Aligns with the SAMHSA Principle of Empowerment, Voice, and Choice: Staff are the facilitators of recovery, and may experience various levels of trauma themselves.

A trauma-informed approach acknowledges that, typically, a privileged class domi-nates conversations and decision-making across settings. This model recognizes that people who have experienced traumatic events often feel as though they have lost power over their own lives, are recipients of coercive treatment, and have historically been diminished in voice and choice.

KEY COMPONENT:
Clients are provided ample, meaningful choice and supported in decision-making and goal-setting.

Clients are provided with as much meaningful choice in the provision of their services as possible. The organization supports clients in shared decision-making and goal-setting.

TID FRAMEWORK

Client Choice and Goal Setting in Sphere I: Policy and Practice

The organization's policies and practices provide clients choice in their services and support them in shared decision-making and goal-setting.

Strategies

The organization supports clients in decision-making related to their services. Staff recognize that individuals who have not had many opportunities to exercise choice may find it difficult or overwhelming, and support them through the process.

The organization's policies and practices prohibit the use of involuntary or coercive practices. Staff do not coerce or punish clients in any way in response to choices that do not align with service goals or recommendations.

Clients feel comfortable engaging in goal-setting and decision-making and feel heard when they do.

Tactics

→ Clients are encouraged to participate in goal-setting.

→ Services reflect the client's preferences, choices, and goals.

→ The organization has a policy that prohibits the use of involuntary or coercive practices.

→ The organization hosts informational sessions about available programs and services for clients, so they can be well-informed when participating in their service plan development.

→ Staff are knowledgeable about the available programs and services, including eligibility requirements, and share this information with clients in an understandable way.

TID FRAMEWORK

→ Staff make themselves available to answer client questions about available programs and services.

Client Choice and Goal Setting in Sphere II: Design Process

The design process is supportive of clients and provides them choices in process and outcome.

Strategies

The design team supports clients through the participatory design process, which leads to insights and feedback that inform the design. Participants are encouraged to participate and advocate for themselves throughout the design process.

The design team incorporates opportunities to generate new ideas or otherwise provide clients options for discussion. Participants are not asked to simply validate ideas but to brainstorm ideas or detail-out designs as part of their collaboration in the design process.

Participatory and collaborative activities leverage various ways of providing input. Participants are able to choose how and when to participate according to their abilities and preferences. The design team provides accommodations for those with disabilities, as well as opportunities to provide input in multiple formats, such as: written and visual; live and asynchronous; and individually and as a team.

Tactics

→ The design team tells participants their experiences afford them a unique perspective, vital in creating a service delivery space that optimizes the client experience.

→ The design is informed by participant insights and feedback.

→ The design team responds to feedback from participants regarding the design process, and makes changes to accommodate the safety and comfort of participants.

→ The design process is iterative and provides multiple opportunities for feedback from participants.

→ The design team explains their decisions regarding the inclusion of feedback to participants. Participants are informed if, and why, any of their recommendations were not included in the final design.

Client Choice and Goal Setting in Sphere III: Built Environment

Clients are provided ample, meaningful choice in the built environment.

Strategies

The built environment includes many opportunities for users to exercise personal choice.

Tactics

→ There are a variety of types and sizes of gathering spaces.

→ There are various types and arrangements of seating and other furnishings.

→ Seating arrangements can be changed by users.

→ Fixed seating arrangements promote various social interaction types so individuals may choose their preferred arrangement.

→ There are adjustable, ergonomic seating and other furnishings.

→ There are adjustable lights.

→ There are a variety of lighting options.

→ There are adjustable window treatments.

→ There are adjustable fans or other air handling features.

→ Users have access to environmental controls such as thermostats and window coverings.

→ Users can adjust the temperature in the spaces they occupy.

→ Users can retreat to areas with noise-mitigation features.

Choice

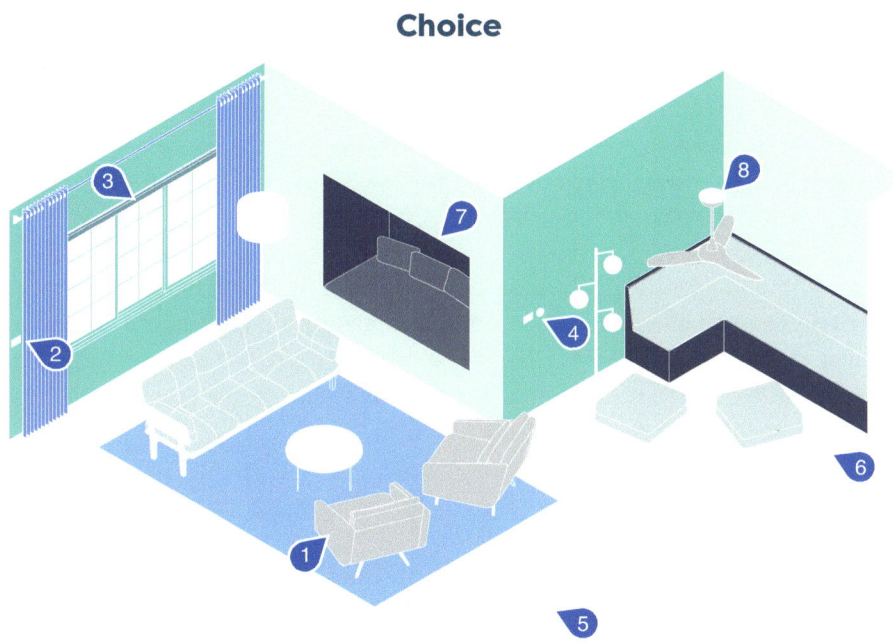

1.	Multiple seating choices	5.	Large open space
2.	Lighting options and controls	6.	Quieter medium space
3.	Ajustable shades and curtains	7.	Small nook
4.	Temperature controls	8.	Controllable ventilation

Illustration by Architecture for Public Benefit

Figure 12. Choice in the built environment

TID FRAMEWORK

DOMAIN 7

EQUITY

Aligns with the SAMHSA Principle of Cultural, Historical, and Gender Awareness: A trauma-informed approach must actively work to identify and dismantle inequities.

When a person experiences inequities, it can have the same negative impact on their long-term health outcomes as other traumas. The impact can be compounded over generations, or when a person is a member of more than one marginalized group. Therefore, a trauma-informed approach inherently works actively to identify and dismantle inequities.

KEY COMPONENT A:
Recognizing and addressing historical trauma supports the empowerment of all people.

Throughout history, our society has been structured in a way that has granted certain privileges to white, cisgender men. Racism is systematically built into our lives on every level, and results in inequities, or barriers, for individuals who are Black, Indigenous, or People of Color (BIPOC). Stereotypes and biases can be based on race, ethnicity, sexual orientation, age, religion, gender identity, geography, and more. A trauma-informed approach recognizes these facts, and is responsive to the gender, racial, ethnic, and cultural needs of clients. It builds relationships that shatter stereotypes and support the empowerment of all people, regardless of to what groups they belong, or may be perceived to belong.

Universal Empowerment in Sphere I: Policy and Practice
The organization's policies and practices recognize and address historical trauma, and support the empowerment of all people.

Strategies
Staff, clients, visitors, and others feel capable and confident to be their authentic selves when interacting with the organization. Staff demonstrate respect for others' culture, traditions, beliefs, religious or spiritual practices, gender and gender expressions, and sexual orientations.

The organization provides regular training or professional development opportunities for staff on JEDI topics. Staff recognize that people from marginalized communities face additional barriers and challenges. They also recognize that people of certain races or ethnicities, or from certain cultures, have endured generations of violence, abuse, and other hardships that impact their ability to meet their needs and are experienced as traumatic.

The organization does not tolerate harassment, bullying, or other hostile environments. It has an anti-discrimination policy and expectations that require staff to demonstrate respect for all people and their cultural practices.

The organization seeks diversity in its staff. When gaps in diversity are identified, the organization seeks perspectives from external partners and sources to fill in potential gaps in cultural understanding.

The organization evaluates its policies and practices with an equity lens, documents inequities and barriers, and attempts to address them.

TID FRAMEWORK

Tactics

→ The organization has a policy that outlines its approach to handling harassing, bullying, and other hostile behavior.

→ The organization uses translation and interpretation services to ensure accessibility for those who may have language access needs.

→ The organization's services are gender-responsive.

→ The program is flexible with rules when necessary to accommodate for barriers that hinder an individual's ability to comply.

→ The organization's services and workforce processes are culturally-responsive and appropriate.

→ The program provides opportunities for clients to express themselves in creative and nonverbal ways (e.g., art, theater, dance, movement, music).

→ Staff at all levels of the program receive training and education on JEDI topics and different cultures (e.g., cultural practices, beliefs, rituals).

Universal Empowerment in Sphere II: Design Process

The design process supports the empowerment of all people. The design team recognizes that research practices have historically taken advantage of minority groups and actively seeks ways to address concerns and provide more inclusive research practices.

Strategies

Staff and participants feel capable and confident to be their authentic selves.
The design team demonstrates respect for others' culture, traditions, beliefs, religious or spiritual practices, gender and gender expressions, and sexual orientations.

TID FRAMEWORK

The design firm provides regular training or professional development opportunities for staff on JEDI topics. The design team members recognize that people from marginalized communities face additional barriers and challenges. They also recognize that people of certain races or ethnicities, or from certain cultures, have endured generations of violence, abuse, and other hardships that impact their ability to meet their needs and are experienced as traumatic.

The design firm does not tolerate harassment, bullying, or other hostile environments. It has an anti-discrimination policy and expectations that require staff to demonstrate respect for all people and their cultural practices.

Participatory design facilitators set ground rules for participants and do not tolerate harassment, bullying, or other hostile environments. The design team members support one another in responding to incidents of harm. If a participant harms another, they are removed from the group until the harm is addressed.

The design team seeks to gain an understanding of the community of users to inform the design. This includes learning what stressors that community might experience as a result of race, ethnicity, gender, culture, or historical trauma. If the design team's process discovers a barrier in the organization or the design, it documents the inequity and attempts to address it.

The design firm seeks diversity in its staff. When gaps in diversity are identified, the organization seeks perspectives from external partners and sources to fill in potential gaps in cultural understanding.

The design firm seeks diversity in its participants and co-designers. The design team recognizes the differences in perspectives that can come with a diverse set of collaborators. The design team actively recruits and encourages participation from marginalized communities. When the design team is unable to include a diverse set of individuals, they recognize and acknowledge limitations in their design processes.

Tactics

→ The design firm has a policy that outlines its approach to handling harassing, bullying, and other hostile behavior.

➜ The design team uses translation and interpretation services to ensure accessibility for those who may have language access needs.

➜ The design team uses written ground rules for participatory design sessions and reviews them with participants before starting each session.

➜ Staff at all levels of the design firm receive training and education on JEDI topics and different cultures (e.g., cultural practices, beliefs, rituals).

➜ The design team reflects on potential biases within their organization, community, or personal belief systems and seeks ways to mitigate these biases from impacting their interactions and research processes.

➜ The design team follows ethical research practices and, when necessary, engages with an independent review board prior to engaging with participants.

➜ Individuals from marginalized communities are included in participatory sessions, the design team, and subcontracting.

Universal Empowerment in Sphere III: Built Environment

The built environment is designed to address historical trauma and support the empowerment of all people.

Strategies

Clients, visitors, staff, and others feel welcome and that they belong in the space.

The design mitigates identified stressors and triggers in the environment.
Think back to the four case studies included in the chapters about the practice of TiD and Sphere I. They are all examples of how using an equity lens to develop an understanding of the situation faced by a marginalized community helped identify stressors in the built environment that could be addressed by design.

TID FRAMEWORK

The design is accessible to all, regardless of their characteristics or abilities.
Members of the LGBTQIA+ community feel safe in the space.

Individuals who are BIPOC feel safe in the space.

Cultural representations in the built environment (e.g., art installations or murals) have been co-developed with individuals from that cultural community.

Tactics

→ The principles of universal design are employed to ensure the space is accessible to all.

→ There are gender-neutral bathrooms for use by clients, visitors, or others.

→ There are gender-neutral bathrooms for staff.

→ Bathrooms are either single units or are closet-style, with floor-to-ceiling partitions.

→ The space includes non-linguistic wayfinding features, such as colors, shapes, or symbols.

KEY COMPONENT B:
Traditional cultural connections have healing value.

Coming together with others that share our culture and lived experience is a powerful salve against historical trauma. This is a form of peer support, in which the group shares similar experiences of living as a marginalized member of society. Learning about other cultures breeds familiarity and fondness. Celebrating cultural traditions together fosters connection, community, and a sense of belonging to those who might otherwise feel othered. The relationships that develop from these connections can then support healing.

TID FRAMEWORK

Fostering Cultural Connections in Sphere I:
Policy and Practice

The organization's policies and practices foster cultural connections.

Strategies

The organization provides opportunities for staff and clients to share their cultures with one another. Recognizing the importance of food in cultural identity, the organization encourages staff and clients to share their traditional and ethnic foods. It hosts events such as potlucks and culture nights, incorporating different types of art and music.

Tactics

→ The organization provides opportunities for clients to lead community events.

→ Clients are encouraged to prepare, have, and share traditional or ethnic foods.

→ The organization sponsors speakers to share cultural traditions.

→ Events hosted by the organization include non-structured time for clients, staff and others to talk freely and get to know one another personally.

Fostering Cultural Connections in Sphere II: Design Process

The design process fosters cultural connections.

Strategies

The design firm provides opportunities for staff to share their cultures with one another. Recognizing the importance of food in cultural identity, the organi-

TID FRAMEWORK

zation encourages staff to share their traditional and ethnic foods. It hosts events such as potlucks and culture nights, incorporating different types of art and music.

The design team encourages participants to share stories about their culture and how it integrates into their daily lives. In addition to building a better cross-cultural understanding, it may lead to insights for the design, such as ways to incorporate spaces that foster cultural traditions and connections.

Tactics

→   The design firm provides opportunities for staff to lead community events.

→   The design firm sponsors speakers to share cultural traditions.

→   Staff are encouraged to prepare, have, and share traditional or ethnic foods.

→   Participatory design sessions include non-structured time for clients, staff, and others to talk freely and get to know one another personally.

→   The design team encourages participants to share stories about their culture and how it integrates into their daily lives.

Fostering Cultural Connections in Sphere III: Built Environment

The built environment fosters cultural connections.

Strategies

The built environment includes spaces designed to foster cultural connec-tions. These spaces should be varied, to accommodate various types of activi-ties and gatherings.

Tactics

→ There are a variety of types and sizes of gathering spaces.

→ There is a large or "teaching" kitchen, in which groups can learn to make cultural or ethnic foods.

→ There are large areas in which cultural dance and other cultural traditions can be taught or experienced.

→ There are cultural representations, meanings, or symbols incorporated into the design that have been created with individuals from that cultural community.

DOMAIN ⑧

COMMUNITY

Aligns with the SAMHSA Principle of Cultural, Historical, Gender Awareness: A trauma-informed approach must actively work to identify and dismantle inequities.

When a person sees elements of themselves reflected back in various aspects of life, they develop a sense of connection and belonging. By seeing people that look like them or share similar cultural traits across settings, they start to identify expanded possibilities for themselves.

When individuals feel as though they belong to a community, they can develop relationships and feel safe taking risks and showing vulnerability. They feel empowered to do so, because they know that they are not relegated to specific roles. By stepping out of their comfort zone, they can acquire new coping strategies and resiliency skills.

KEY COMPONENT:
Incorporating and reflecting the community's culture promotes a sense of belonging.

Clients and staff who see themselves and their culture reflected in the world around them are more likely to develop a sense of belonging, which is a key element in building resiliency.

Cultural Reflection in Sphere I: Policy and Practice

The organization's policies and practices reflect the race, ethnicity, and culture of clients and staff.

Strategies

The organization reflects the racial, ethnic, and cultural backgrounds of clients and the local community in its choice of art, furnishings, and resources.

The staff is proportionally representative of their clients' racial, ethnic, and cultural backgrounds.

Tactics

→ The organization displays art created by individuals with similar racial, ethnic, and cultural backgrounds to those of clients.

→ The organization plays music created by individuals with similar racial, ethnic, and cultural backgrounds to those of clients.

→ The organization uses books and other resources and materials created by individuals with similar racial, ethnic, and cultural backgrounds to those of clients.

→ The organization features quotes by, the discoveries of, and other notable facts about, individuals with similar racial, ethnic, and cultural backgrounds to those of clients throughout its space.

→ The organization purchases from locally-owned businesses and service providers.

→ The organization uses patterns, colors, and symbols that reflect the racial, ethic, and cultural backgrounds of clients and the local community.

Cultural Reflection in Sphere II: Design Process

The design process reflects the race, ethnicity, and culture of clients and staff.

Strategies

During the participatory design process, the design team displays and incorporates patterns, colors, and symbols that reflect the racial, ethnic, and cultural backgrounds of clients and the local community.

The design team encourages feedback from participants on uplifting and relevant figures, patterns, colors, and symbols that reflect the racial, ethnic, and cultural backgrounds of clients and the local community. The team incorporates these into the design, and solicits feedback on their inclusion to ensure they are used appropriately.

Tactics

→ Patterns, colors, and symbols that reflect the racial, ethnic, and cultural backgrounds of clients and the local community have been informed by the clients and local community themselves.

→ The design team shares similar racial, ethnic, and cultural backgrounds to those of clients.

Cultural Reflection in Sphere III: Built Environment

The built environment reflects the race, ethnicity, and culture of clients and staff.

Strategies

The built environment reflects the racial, ethnic, and cultural backgrounds of clients, the local community, and staff in its choice of art, fixtures, and furnishings.

TID FRAMEWORK

Tactics

→ The art used throughout the space is created by individuals with similar racial, ethnic, and cultural backgrounds to those of clients.

→ The art used throughout the space represents the full diversity of the population.

→ The built environment features quotes by, the discoveries of, and other notable facts about, individuals with similar racial, ethnic, and cultural backgrounds to those of clients throughout its space.

→ The built environment includes patterns, colors, and symbols that reflect the racial, ethic, and cultural backgrounds of, or are otherwise related to, clients and the local community.

→ Clients', staff's, and the community's cultures are incorporated into the design (e.g., tile work, patterns, sculptures, paths).

→ The space incorporates locally-produced materials.

→ Materials are purchased from minority-owned businesses.

→ Installation and construction are serviced by local and/or minority-owned organizations.

DOMAIN

COMFORT

Aligns with the SAMHSA Principle of Safety: Throughout the organization, staff and the people they serve feel physically and psychologically safe.

When a person is comfortable, they feel safe and their stress levels are buffered. A trauma-informed environment is therefore be built around the comfort of the people who will be using the space. Design choices should include a focus on features that can increase enjoyment and a sense of ease.

KEY COMPONENT:
Ease, familiarity, and hominess contribute to comfort.

Creating a sense of ease, familiarity, and hominess lead to comfort in the environment or with the interactions taking place.

Ease, Familiarity, and Hominess in Sphere I:
Policy and Practice

The organization's policies and practices foster a sense of ease, familiarity, and hominess.

TID FRAMEWORK

Strategies

The organization employs routines. In recognition of the fact that many individuals, including those who have experienced trauma, feel safer when they know what to expect, services and activities follow predictable patterns. When changes are necessary, they are communicated to clients and staff as soon as possible.

Tactics

➜ Schedules and services delivery are predictable and reliable.

Ease, Familiarity, and Hominess in Sphere II: Design Process

The design process fosters a sense of ease, familiarity, and hominess.

Strategies

The design team is transparent about its processes, expectations, timelines, limitations, and deliverables. When changes are necessary, the team communicates them to participants as soon as possible.

The space in which participatory design sessions are held is welcoming and features relaxing elements. Biophilic patterns that can positively impact mental health, mood, tranquility, and comfort are included in the design. These include visual, non-visual, and material connection to nature, the presence of water, and prospect.

Tactics

➜ The design process is clear and predictable.

➜ There are visual, non-visual, and material connections with nature in, or accessible from, the participatory design space.

→ There are water features in the participatory design space.

→ There are areas in the participatory design space where a person can view who is present and what is happening from a distance.

→ Participants are provided the opportunity to take a break at any time.

Ease, Familiarity, and Hominess in Sphere III: Built Environment

The built environment fosters a sense of ease, familiarity, and hominess.

Strategies

The built environment is welcoming and evokes a sense of ease, familiarity, and home. Creating an environment that is accessible and reflective of environments users are familiar with facilitates comprehension of, and comfort with, a new space.

Biophilic patterns that can positively impact mental health, mood, tranquility, and comfort are included in the design. These include visual, non-visual, and material connection to nature, the presence of water, and prospect.

Tactics

→ The space complies with accessibility standards.

→ The furnishings align with the general cultural aesthetic preferences of the population of users.

→ Colors, patterns, imagery, and textures identified as soothing to the population of users are used throughout the space.

→ There are visual, non-visual, and material connections with nature in, or accessible from, the space.

➔ There are water features in the space.

➔ There are areas in the space where a person can view who is present and what is happening from a distance.

DOMAIN ⑩

MOVEMENT

Aligns with the Polyvagal theory: Humans regulate their nervous systems through three main circuits that create six physiological states.

People with a high heart rate variability are more resilient to stress. We can reduce the reactivity of our autonomic nervous system (ANS) and increase our window of tolerance by engaging in movement. Activities that involve movement and social engagement are even more beneficial. Still, in keeping with the principle of Empowerment and Voice, individuals should never feel forced into movement.

KEY COMPONENT:
Movement can help regulate the nervous system and enhance learning and healing processes.

By understanding the polyvagal theory and what types of activities can impact the ANS, we can encourage movement, to expand the window of tolerance of staff, clients, visitors, and others, and help them better regulate when stressed.

Movement in Sphere I: Policy and Practice

The organization's policies and practices encourage movement.

Strategies

The organization plans for and encourages movement and breaks. Staff and clients are provided with wellness resources that explain the benefits of movement, including yoga and stretching, as a means of regulating and attaining better health outcomes.

Tactics

→   Staff are provided with resources that explain the benefits of movement.

→   Services and meetings incorporate time and space for movement breaks.

→   Staff are provided benefits that encourage movement, such as discounts for wellness centers or gyms.

Movement in Sphere II: Design Process

The design process encourages movement.

Strategies

The design process plans for movement and breaks. Team members encourage participants to stretch or move about as a way of regulating and refreshing after focused work.

The design firm plans for and encourages movement and breaks. Staff are provided with wellness resources that explain the benefits of movement, including yoga and stretching, as a means of regulating and attaining better health outcomes.

Through the participatory design process, the design team identifies ways to encourage movement in the design that appeal to the community of users.

During collaborative sessions, participants are provided ways to elicit or assess ideas through movement.

Tactics

→ Design team work spaces include seating options that offer movement opportunities (e.g., rocking chairs, wobble stools, balance balls).

→ Participants engage in movement and take breaks during design sessions.

→ Design team meetings incorporate time and space for movement breaks.

→ The design includes appealing enticements to movement.

Movement in Sphere III: Built Environment

The built environment encourages movement.

Strategies

There are features throughout the built environment that encourage movement. These features should include variability to allow for choice and accommodate for those with mobility concerns.

There are features throughout the built environment that encourage social engagement while moving. This may include making music with others, especially singing, playing games, or petting or walking an animal.

Tactics

→ Stairs are well-lit, aesthetically pleasing, and prominently featured in main access areas.

→ There are seating options that offer movement opportunities (e.g., rocking chairs, wobble stools, balance balls).

→ There are swings or hammocks in the space.

→ There are play areas or climbing structures within the built environment or on the grounds.

→ There are walking paths or trails on, or near, the grounds.

→ There is storage near the entrance for bike and scooter storage.

→ There are oversized musical instruments built into, the environment.

→ There are rooms in which people can make music.

→ There are pet-friendly areas. As pets are rarely stationary, they encourage the people with them to move throughout the space.

→ Games are incorporated into the built environment (e.g., life-sized chess boards, bean-bag toss).

→ There are playing fields on, or near, the grounds.

DOMAIN  11

PLAY

Aligns with Play and Polyvagal theories: Play is necessary to develop healthy attachments, emotional intelligence, and strong relationships. Humans regulate their nervous systems through three main circuits that create six physiological states.

Play enhances our ability to learn, helps us understand social boundaries, and increases health and well-being. It is a building block in learning how to develop healthy relationships, which are essential in protecting against the harmful effects of trauma. Along with dance, sports, and performance, play is an active expression of pleasurable social engagement.

Based on the concepts of play theory, we recognize that play environments should be inviting, excite curiosity, and include natural features and opportunities for sensory exploration to support learning and the development of crucial relationship-strengthening skills, including cooperation, communication, negotiation, social skills, and empathy.

KEY COMPONENT:
Play is a building block in learning how to develop healthy relationships.

Infants develop attunement with their caregivers through early play. This helps them form a healthy attachment style and learn how their actions can impact others. As they age, they can test and learn physical and social boundaries through play with peers and others, developing emotional intelligence and social well-being over time.

Play in Sphere I: Policy and Practice

The organization's policies and practices encourage play.

Strategies

The organization incorporates and encourages play. Play is built into service delivery whenever possible and staff are encouraged to engage in play during breaks. Staff and clients are provided with wellness resources that explain the benefits of play.

Tactics

→   Services regularly include play.

→   Staff and clients are provided with wellness resources that explain the benefits of play.

Play in Sphere II: Design Process

The design process encourages play.

Strategies

The design process incorporates play. Participatory design processes lend themselves to playful exercises especially well. These can include role-playing and exercises in which participants are asked to play the fairy godmother and waive their "magic wand" to design their imagined perfect space.

The design firm encourages play. Staff are provided with wellness resources that explain the benefits of play, as well as materials to engage in playful activities.

Through the participatory design process, the design team identifies ways to encourage play in the design that appeal to the community of users.

Tactics

→ Design team meetings incorporate time and space for play.

→ Design team members are provided with materials to engage in arts, crafts, or play (e.g., adult coloring books, yarn, puzzles).

→ Collaborative sessions include warm-up and cool-down activities that allow participants to play and have a mental break before and after focused work.

→ Participants engage in playful activities during design sessions.

→ The design includes appealing enticements to play.

Play in Sphere III: Built Environment
The built environment encourages play.

Strategies
There are features throughout the built environment that encourage play.

Biophilic patterns that produce a sense of pleasure are included in the design. These include mystery and risk/peril, which introduces an identifiable threat with a reliable safeguard.

TID FRAMEWORK

Tactics

→ There are elements in the design that are interesting to the senses.

→ There are interesting art features present.

→ There are intentional variations within ceiling height and features.

→ Games are incorporated into the built environment (e.g., chess, checkers, and other game boards; blackboard paint and chalk; "I spy" games with visual icons of things to find in the environment; a "secret wall" where users can leave anonymous, unread notes).

→ There are play areas or climbing structures within the built environment or on the grounds.

→ There are natural elements within the built environment that encourage climbing or play (e.g., boulders, hills, linked logs).

→ There are playing fields on, or near, the grounds.

→ There are musical instruments, either available for use, or built into, the environment.

→ There are rooms in which people can make music.

→ There are elements in the design that allow a person to take exciting and enjoyable risks, with the assurance of safety features (e.g., slide, zipline, play area).

→ There are elements in the design that create intrigue by hinting at more information to be discovered. This is often achieved through partially obscured views or other sensory devices that entice the individual to travel deeper into the environment.

CONCLUSION

THE TID FRAMEWORK PROVIDED IN THIS BOOK IS NOT INTENDED as a checklist for TiD practitioners. Instead, it serves as a structure practitioners can use when engaging in projects, to ensure that they are trauma-informed in all three spheres of TiD: policy and practice, design process, and the built environment.

In order to truly engage in TiD, practitioners need to understand the concepts, theories, and evidence presented in these pages, and apply them throughout all stages of their work. When applying TiD with fidelity, evidence suggests that practitioners should be able to create environments that reduce the stress levels of occupants, resulting in long-term health improvements. The resulting designs would maximize choice, and create a safe, comfortable environment for clients and staff, and help users develop a sense of safety, where they can build resilience, strengthen their ability to emotionally regulate, and better access new opportunities.

Trauma-informed Design is a burgeoning field of practice that will continue to evolve in the coming years. Recognizing this, we intend to update this reference as new evidence and information alters and expands best practices in the TiD approach. Practitioners are encouraged to reach out to the TiD Society to provide feedback or information based on their experiences for consideration in upcoming revisions.

APPENDIX A:
TRAUMA-INFORMED LANGUAGE CHOICES

Below are some examples of trauma-informed language choices. This list is not exhaustive, but intended to provide a start for individuals seeking to shift to more trauma-informed language. Although "individual" is used throughout the examples, it can be replaced with other similar words, such as "person" or "client."

Instead Of	Use
Homeless	Unhoused; Individual living with insecure housing
Slave	Enslaved person
Victim	Survivor; individual who experienced _____
Rape victim	Survivor of sexual assault; individual who was raped
Drug (ab)user; addict; junkie	Individual affected by (or engaging in) drug use; Individual with an addiction
Drunk; alcohol abuser; substance abuser	Individual with a substance use disorder
Schizophrenic/depressive/bipolar	Individual who has been diagnosed with schizophrenia/depression/bipolar disorder
High(er) risk group; groups with high-risk behavior	High-risk behavior; highly affected communities; key populations at higher-risk
Catch (an infection)	Contract; become infected with
Sexually transmitted disease (STD)	Sexually transmitted infection (STI)
Risky sex	Unprotected sex

Instead Of	Use
Promiscuous	Having multiple partners
Prostitute; hooker	Sex worker; individual involved in transactional sex
Non-compliant, unmotivated; resistant (to treatment)	Opted not to; has not begun; experiencing ambivalence and change
Committed suicide	Died by suicide; completed suicide
Stakeholder	Invested party
Immigrant	Migrant; foreign national; New American
Illegal immigrant	Resident without legal permission; individual without proper documentation
Defendant	Individual facing charges; individual awaiting trial/sentencing
Inmate; prisoner	Individual who is incarcerated
Probationer; parolee; furloughee	Individual under supervision; individual on probation/parole/furlough
Criminal; offender	Individual who engaged in criminalized behavior; individual who is involved in the criminal legal system; individual who is justice-involved
Ex-offender; ex-inmate; ex-felon; ex-con, ex-convict	Individual who was incarcerated; individual with lived experience of incarceration; returning citizen

APPENDIX B:
GLOSSARY

Attunement: A caregiver's ability to recognize and respond to their child's needs.

Cisgender: A person whose current gender identity corresponds to the sex they were assigned at birth.

Collective trauma: A significant traumatic event that shatters the basic fabric of a society.

Cultural: The shared behaviors, beliefs, values, and symbols characteristic of a particular group of people, as a social, ethnic, professional, or age group.

Culturally-responsive: A strengths-based approach that acknowledges and respects the role of culture in a person's beliefs, attitudes, and behaviors. It is built on the recognition that a person's background and culture affect their values, language, norms, and day-to-day life. Culturally-responsive services incorporate and center the unique experiences and identities of the individuals being served in their service-delivery.

Disparate impact: An adverse effect on a group of people, as compared to others.

Dose-response relationship: A relationship in which altering the amount of exposure to a stimulus or stressor results in a corresponding response in an individual (e.g., increasing exposure results in increased effects). The more trauma a person experiences, the more they are likely to have lasting, negative impacts.

Equity: Ensuring access to resources that allow all people the opportunity to survive and thrive across groups, in spite of systemic barriers.

Gender expression: How a person enacts or expresses their gender in everyday life and within the context of their culture and society. Expression of gender through physical appearance may include dress, hairstyle, accessories, cosmetics, hormonal, and surgical interventions as well as mannerisms, speech, behavioral patterns, and names. A person's gender expression may or may not conform to a person's gender identity.

Gender identity: A person's deeply felt, internal, intrinsic sense of their own gender. Gender identity may or may not be aligned with a person's sex assigned at birth. Gender identity focuses on how a person identifies themselves, not on how others may perceive them.

Gender-responsive: Recognizing and accounting for the important differences among genders in psychological development, socialization culture, exposure to trauma, and life experiences. Gender responsive practices are relational, trauma-informed, strength-based, and culturally-relevant.

Harm: Physical, psychological, or emotional injury, suffering, or pain.

Holistic: The treatment of the whole person, taking into account factors, including those that are environmental, mental, social, and cultural, rather than just symptoms or behaviors.

Impact: The effect or influence of a person, thing, or action, regardless of intent.

Inclusive: An environment in which there are diverse members, all members are welcomed, their ideas, needs, and ways of being are honored, and power is shared.

Intergenerational trauma: When a parent passes the effects of their own trauma onto their children, often because their trauma keeps them from sufficiently meeting their children's needs.

Justice: The mechanisms, processes, and outcomes that ensure an equitable and restorative resolution to harm for all involved.

Language access: The use of relevant resources (e.g., translation, interpreters) to facilitate the ease of clear, accurate, and understandable communication across all linguistic abilities, languages, and cultures.

Lived experience: Knowledge based on a person's perspective, personal identities, and history, beyond their professional or educational experience.

Marginalized group: Peoples, populations, groups, or communities that experience disparate impact across systems and institutions because of unequal power relationships across economic, political, social, and cultural dimensions.

Religion: A set of beliefs or practices concerning the cause, nature, and purpose of the universe, especially when considered as the creation of a superhuman agency or agencies, usually involving devotional and ritual observances, and often containing a moral code governing the conduct of human affairs.

Sexual orientation: Refers to a person's sexual identity, attractions, and behaviors in relation to people on the basis of their gender(s) and/or sex characteristics.

Social capital: The value derived from positive connections between people. This is often in the form of a network of relationships among people who live and work in a particular society, enabling that society to function effectively.

Social determinates (or influences) of health: Nonmedical factors that influence health outcomes. They are the conditions in which people are born, grow, work, live, and age. These forces and systems include a wide set of forces and systems that shape daily life such as economic policies and systems, development agendas, social norms, social policies, and political systems.

Survivor: A person with who has lived through a traumatic experience.

Systemic barriers: Obstacles that collectively affect a group disproportionately and perpetuate or maintain disparities in outcomes. Structural barriers can be policies, practices, and other norms that favor an advantaged group while systematically disadvantaging another group.

Trauma: Trauma results from an event, series of events, or set of circumstances that is experienced by an individual as physically or emotionally harmful or threatening and that has lasting adverse effects on the individual's functioning and physical, social, emotional, or spiritual well-being. Trauma can result from acute, chronic, developmental, generational, cultural, or systemic experiences.

Trauma-informed: A program, organization, or system that realizes the widespread impact of trauma and understands potential paths for recovery; recognizes the signs and symptoms of trauma in clients, families, staff, and others involved with the system; responds by fully integrating knowledge about trauma into policies, procedures, and practices; and seeks to actively resist re-traumatization.

Trigger: A stimulus that sets off a memory of a trauma or a specific portion of a traumatic experience.

Vulnerable populations: Populations which are at greater risk, as a result of their actual or perceived identity or health, including physical, behavioral, or mental, for disparate outcomes compared to the general population. This can be based on physical, social, economical, racial, ethnic, cultural, or other factors.ing-and-cul-tural-strategies-to-resist-displacement

REFERENCES

Anda, R. F., Porter, L. E., & Brown, D. W. (2020). Inside the adverse childhood experience score: Strengths, limitations, and misapplications. *American Journal of Preventive Medicine, 59*(2), 293-295, https://doi.org/10.1016/j.amepre.2020.01.009

Arellano, L. (2022). Questioning the science: How quantitative methodologies perpetuate inequity in higher education. *Education Sciences, 12*(2), 116. https://doi.org/10.3390/educsci12020116

Benjet, C., Bromet, E., Karam, E. G., Kessler, R. C., McLaughlin, K. A., Ruscio, A. M., Shahly, V., Stein, D. J., Petukhova, M., Hill, E., Alonso, J., Atwoli, L., Bunting, B., Bruffaerts, R., Caldas-de-Almeida, J. M., de Girolamo, G., Florescu, S., Gureje, O., Huang, Y., & Koenen, K. C. (2016). The epidemiology of traumatic event exposure worldwide: Results from the world mental health survey consortium. *Psychological Medicine, 46*(2), 327-343. https://doi.org/10.1017/S0033291715001981

Bethell, C., Jones, J., Gombojav, N., Linkenbach, J., & Sege, R. (2019). Positive childhood experiences and adult mental and relational health in a statewide sample: Associations across adverse childhood experiences levels. *JAMA Pediatrics. 173*(11), e193007-e193007. https://doi:10.1001/jamapediatrics.2019.3007

Bonumwezi, J. L., Grapin, S. L., Uddin, M., Coyle, S., Habintwali, D., & Lowe, S. (2024). Intergenerational trauma transmission through family psychosocial factors in adult children of Rwandan survivors of the 1994 genocide against the Tutsi, *Social Science & Medicine, 348*, 116837, https://doi.org/10.1016/j.socscimed.2024.116837

Brandt, A. M. (1978). Racism and research: The case of the Tuskegee Syphilis Study. *Hastings Center Report,* 21-29, http://nrs.harvard.edu/urn-3:HUL.InstRepos:3372911

Browning, W.D., Ryan, C.O., & Clancy, J.O. (2014, 2024). *14 Patterns of Biophilic Design.* (10th Anniversary Edition, 2024). Terrapin Bright Green, LLC. https://www.terrapinbrightgreen.com/report/14-patterns/

Centers for Disease Control and Prevention (CDC). (2021). *Behavioral risk factor surveillance system.* [Data set]. U.S. Department of Health and Human Services, Centers for Disease Control and Prevention. https://www.cdc.gov/brfss/index.html

Centers for Disease Control and Prevention (CDC). (2013). *Health effects of gentrification.* U.S. Department of Health and Human Services, Centers for Disease Control and Prevention. http://medbox.iiab.me/modules/en-cdc/www.cdc.gov/healthyplaces/healthtopics/gentrification.htm

Centers for Disease Control and Prevention (CDC). (2024, January 17). *Social determinants of health (SDOH).* U.S. Department of Health and Human Services, Centers for Disease Control and Prevention. https://www.cdc.gov/about/priorities/why-is-addressing-sdoh-important.html

Child Development Institute. (2018). *The power of attunement.* https://cdikids.org/autism/power-attunement/#:~:text=Attunement%20is%20our%20ability%20to,quality%20of%20their%20emotional%20relationship

Cipan, V. (2023, March 29). *What is participatory design and what makes it great?* Point Jupiter - Web development and UX design agency. https://pointjupiter.com/what-is-participatory-design-what-makes-it-great/

Cleveland Clinic. (2024a, May 1). *Adrenaline: Where the hormone is located & what it does.* https://my.clevelandclinic.org/health/body/23038-adrenaline

Cleveland Clinic. (2024b, May 1). *Cortisol: What it is, function, symptoms & levels.* https://my.clevelandclinic.org/health/articles/22187-cortisol

Cleveland Clinic. (2024c, June 27). *Norepinephrine: What it is, function, deficiency & side effects.* https://my.clevelandclinic.org/health/articles/22610-norepinephrine-noradrenaline

Costa, D. L., Yetter, N., & DeSomer, H. (2018). Intergenerational transmission of paternal trauma among US Civil War ex-POWs. *Proceedings of the National Academy of Sciences, 115*(44), 11215-11220. https://doi.org/10.1073/pnas.1803630115

Dietkus, R. (2022). The call for trauma-informed design research and practice. *Design Management Review, 33*(2), 26-31. https://onlinelibrary.wiley.com/doi/10.1111/drev.12295

Dias, B. G., & Ressler, K. J. (2014). Parental olfactory experience influences behavior and neural structure in subsequent generations. *Nature Neuroscience, 17*(1), 89–96. https://doi.org/10.1038/nn.3594

Dovetail Editorial Team. (2023, July 9). *Participatory design: Definition, methods, and implementation*. Dovetail. https://dovetail.com/ux/participatory-design/

Elizarova, O., & Dowd, K. (2017, December 14). *Participatory design in practice*. UX Magazine. https://uxmag.com/articles/participatory-design-in-practice

Ellis, W. R., & Dietz, W. H. (2017). A new framework for addressing adverse childhood and community experiences: The building community resilience (BCR) model. *Academic Pediatrics, 17*(7) S86-S93. https://doi:10.1016/j.acap.2016.12.011

Fagen, R. & Fagen, J. (2009). Play behaviour and multi-year juvenile survival in free-ranging brown bears, Ursus arctos. *Evolutionary Ecology Research 11*(7). 1053-1067. https://www.evolutionary-ecology.com/abstracts/v11/2446.html

Fallot, R. D., & Harris, M. (n.d.). Trauma-informed program self-assessment scale Version 1.4 (5-06): *Community Connections*. https://www.theannainstitute.org/TIPSASCORESHEET.pdf

Farkas, M. (2019). Process matters in design: Using participatory design to include stakeholders. American Libraries, 50(9/10),56. https://americanlibrariesmagazine.org/2019/09/03/process-matters-participatory-design/

Felitti, V. J., Anda, R. F., Nordenberg, D., Williamson, D. F., Spitz, A. M., Edwards, V., & Marks, J. S. (1998). Relationship of childhood abuse and household dysfunction to many of the leading causes of death in adults: The Adverse Childhood Experiences (ACE) Study. *American Journal of Preventive Medicine, 14*(4), 245-258. https://doi.org/10.1016/S0749-3797(98)00017-8

Ford, T. N., & Goger, A. (2021, October 14). *The value of qualitative data for advancing equity in policy.* Brookings. https://www.brookings.edu/articles/value-of-qualitative-data-for-advancing-equity-in-policy

Goodyear-Brown, P. (2019). *Trauma and play therapy: Helping children heal.* Routledge.

Guarino, K., Soares, P., Konnath, K., Clervil, R., & Bassuk, E. (2021, August 11). *Trauma-informed organizational toolkit for Homeless Services.* Center for Mental Health Services, Substance Abuse and Mental Health Services Administration, and the Daniels Fund, the National Child Traumatic Stress Network, and the W.K. Kellogg Foundation. https://traumainformedoregon.org/tic-resources/trauma-informed-organizational-toolkit-homeless-services/

Harvard Health Publishing Staff. (2024, April 3). *Heart rate variability: How it might indicate well-being.* Harvard Health Publishing: Harvard Medical School. https://www.health.harvard.edu/blog/heart-rate-variability-new-way-track-well-2017112212789

Health Resources and Services Administration Maternal and Child Health Bureau. (2020, June). *Adverse childhood experiences NSCH data brief.* https://mchb.hrsa.gov/sites/default/files/mchb/data-research/nsch-ace-databrief.pdf

Hummer, V. & Dollard, N. (2010). *Creating trauma-informed care environments: An organizational self-assessment (part of Creating Trauma-Informed Care Environments curriculum).* The Department of Child & Family Studies within the College of Behavioral and Community Sciences, University of South Florida.

Interaction Design Foundation. (2024, March 1). *What is participatory design? - updated 2024.* The Interaction Design Foundation. https://www.interaction-design.org/literature/topics/participatory-design#:~:text=Participatory%20design%20is%20a%20collaborative,applying%20their%20knowledge%20and%20experiences.

ioby. (2023, July 28). *ioby's comprehensive guide to creative placekeeping.* ioby. https://ioby.org/resources/iobys-comprehensive-guide-to-creative-placekeeping/

Jones, S. (2024, June 23). *Why sensorial work is so important in Montessori.* Montessori for Today. https://montessorifortoday.com/why-sensorial-work-is-so-important-in-montessori/

Kilpatrick, D. G., Resnick, H. S., Milanak, M. E., Miller, M. W., Keyes, K. M., & Friedman, M. J. (2013). National estimates of exposure to traumatic events and PTSD prevalence using DSM-IV and DSM-5 criteria. *Journal of Traumatic Stress, 26*(5), 537-547. https://doi.org/10.1002/jts.21848

Kopec, D. & Harte, J. D. (2020). 'Design as the missing variable in trauma-informed schools'. In E. Rossen (Ed.), *Supporting and educating traumatized students:*
A guide for school-based professionals (pp. 343-357). Oxford University Press.

Lanier, P. (2020, July 2). *Racism is an adverse childhood experience (ACE).* School of Social Work, Jordan Institute for Families. https://jordaninstituteforfamilies.org/2020/racism-is-an-adverse-childhood-experience-ace/

Maynard, T., & Waters, J. (2014). *Exploring outdoor play in the early years.* McGraw-Hill Education.

Merrick, B. (2022, November 23). Friedrich Froebel. Early Education. https://early-education.org.uk/friedrich-froebel/

McLeod, S. (2024a, January 25). *Erik Erikson's stages of psychosocial development*. Simply Psychology. https://www.simplypsychology.org/erik-erikson.html

McLeod, S. (2024b, August 5). *Piaget's Theory and stages of cognitive development*. Simply Psychology. https://www.simplypsychology.org/piaget.html

National Council for Behavioral Health. (n.d.). *Organizational self-assessment: Adoption of trauma-informed care approaches in a primary care setting (TIPC-OSA)*. https://www.thenationalcouncil.org/wp-content/uploads/2022/04/OSA-Tutorial.pdf

National Institute for Play. (2024, May 20). https://nifplay.org/

Peavey, E. K., & Ames, R. L. (2025). Designing for peace through a trauma-informed perspective. In M. M. C. Shepley (Ed.), *Peace by design* (pp. 56–82). Routledge.

Perroud, N., Rutembesa, E., Paoloni-Giacobino, A., Mutabaruka, J., Mutesa, L., Stenz, L., Malafosse, A., & Karege, F. (2014). The Tutsi genocide and transgenerational transmission of maternal stress: Epigenetics and biology of the HPA axis. *The World Journal of Biological Psychiatry, 15*(4), 334-345. https://doi:10.3109/15622975.2013.866693

Polyvagal Institute. (n.d.). *What is polyvagal theory?* https://www.polyvagalinstitute.org/whatispolyvagaltheory

Porges, S. (2020). *Trauma through the lens of polyvagal theory*. Trauma Research Foundation's Certificate in Traumatic Stress Studies. https://traumaresearchfoundation.org/programs/certificate-program/

Reggio Emilia Early Learning Centre. (2024). *How the Reggio Emilia approach nurtures a child's well-being*. https://reggioemilia.com.au/blog/how-the-reggio-emilia-approach-nurtures-a-childs-well-being/#:~:text=In%20this%20program%2C%20families%20are,ability%20to%20form%20meaningful%20relationships

Santoro, H. (2023). *The push for more equitable research is changing the field.* Monitor on Psychology. https://www.apa.org/monitor/2023/01/trends-inclusivity-psychological-research

Siegel, D. J. (1999). *The developing mind: How relationships and the brain interact to shape who we are.* Guilford Press.

Sims, J. M. (2010). A brief review of the Belmont report. *Dimensions of Critical Care Nursing, 29*(4), 173-174. https://doi.10.1097/DCC.0b013e3181de9ec5

Skloot, R. (2017). *The immortal life of Henrietta Lacks.* Broadway Paperbacks.

Southern Poverty Law Center (SPLC). (n.d.). Common beliefs survey: Teaching racially and ethnically diverse students. *Learning for Justice.* https://www.learningforjustice.org/professional-development/common-beliefs-survey-teaching-racially-and-ethnically-diverse-students

St. George, S. M., Harkness, A. R., Rodriguez-Diaz, C. E., Weinstein, E. R., Pavia, V., & Hamilton, A. B. (2023). Applying rapid qualitative analysis for health equity: Lessons learned using "EARS" with Latino communities. *International Journal of Qualitative Methods, 22,* https://doi.org/10.1177/16094069231164938

Substance Abuse and Mental Health Services Administration (SAMHSA). (2023). *Practical guide for implementing a trauma-informed approach.* https://store.samhsa.gov/sites/default/files/pep23-06-05-005.pdf

Substance Abuse and Mental Health Services Administration (SAMHSA). (2014). *SAMHSA's concept of trauma and guidance for a trauma-informed approach.* https://ncsacw.acf.hhs.gov/userfiles/files/SAMHSA_Trauma.pdf

Swedo, E. A., Aslam, M. V., Dahlberg, L. L., Niolon, P. H., Guinn, A. S., Simon, T. R., Mercy, J. A. (2023). Prevalence of adverse childhood experiences among U.S. adults — behavioral risk factor surveillance system, 2011–2020. *Morbidity and Mortality Weekly Report, 72*(26), 707-715. http://dx.doi.org/10.15585/mmwr.mm7226a2

Thrive Initiative. (2011). *Trauma-informed agency assessment: System of care trauma-informed agency assessment.* https://www.maine.gov/dhhs/sites/maine.gov.dhhs/files/documents/ocfs/cbhs/webinars/documents/SOC-TIAA-Family.pdf

van der Kolk, B. (2015). *The body keeps the score: Brain, mind, and body in the healing of trauma* (Reprint ed). Penguin Publishing Group

Walker, P. (n.d.). *The 4Fs: A trauma typology in complex PTSD.* Psychotherapy. https://pete-walker.com/fourFs_TraumaTypologyComplexPTSD.htm#:~:text=Complex%20PTSD%20as%20an%20Attachment%20Disorder&text=Emotional%20Flashbacks%20are%20instant%20and,%2C%20grief%20and%2For%20depression

WellMind Counselling (2024, August 6). *How to identify CPTSD/emotional flashbacks and triggers and what to do when one happens.* https://www.wellmind.ca/post/cptsd-emotional-flashback-what-to-do#:~:text=What%20is%20a%20CPTSD%20Flashback?%20A%20CPTSD,traumatic%20events%2C%20CPTSD%20flashbacks%20are%20commonly%20emotion%2Dbased

World Health Organization (WHO). (n.d.). *Social determinants of health.* World Health Organization. https://www.who.int/health-topics/social-determinants-of-health#tab=tab_1

Yehuda, R., Daskalakis, N. P., Bierer, L. M., Bader, H. N., Klengel, T., Holsboer, F., & Binder, E. B. (2016). Holocaust exposure induced intergenerational effects on FKBP5 methylation. *Biological Psychiatry, 80*(5), 372-380. https://doi:10.1016/j.biopsych.2015.08.005

Yu, B., Lowenstein, D., & Bedoya, R. (2016, March 8). *Creative placemaking, placekeeping, and cultural strategies to resist displacement.* US Department of Arts and Culture. https://usdac.us/blogac/2017/12/11/creative-placemaking-placekeeping-and-cultural-strategies-to-resist-displacement

ABOUT THE AUTHORS

CHRISTINE ANN AWAD COWART, MA

Christine Ann Awad Cowart, a dually certified trauma professional has built a career in the human services field, with a focus on criminal legal systems and family services policy. After earning her Master of Criminal Justice degree from the State University of New York at Albany, Christine was employed as a state legislative analyst in New York, and then New Jersey. She has also worked as a policy analyst for the New York State Division of Parole and a contract and grant specialist for the Vermont Department for Children and Families, where she doubled as the co-chair for the Family Services Division's racial equity workgroup. She currently serves as the policy director for the Vermont Department of Corrections, where she is helping to implement a Department-wide trauma-informed approach.

Christine was raised in the United States by two immigrant parents, one from North Africa, the other from Waestern Europe, who merged the best of their vastly different cultures. After marrying, she joyfully welcomed two Indigenous sons from South America, each with their own personalities, stories, gifts, and traumatic histories. Her personal and professional experiences led her to a clear recognition of trauma and its effects throughout our society and what can be done to change the story. Driven to research and share this information, Christine founded Cowart Trauma Informed Partnership, to help individuals and organizations implement trauma-informed practices.

Recognizing that the physical spaces in which we spend time can impact our perceptions, stress levels, and ability to regulate our emotional responses and behaviors, Christine joined Janet E. Roche and J. Davis Harte as a co-founder of the Trauma-informed Design Society, in 2021.

JANET E. ROCHE, MDS, CAPS

Janet E. Roche, MDS CAPS is a leader in designing for health and wellness. She received her Masters in Design for Human Health within the Masters of Design Studies program at the Boston Architectural College (BAC). Immediately following graduation she has been an adjunct BAC instructor teaching: Environmental Health, Human Conditions + Design, and Biophilia. She mentors BAC students in a various work-study programs to examine, among other things, health determinants with in the built environment.

Janet is also currently the Chair for the Alumni Council for the BAC. With a background with a B.S. in Social Work from Boston University, her Certificate of Business and Management from Harvard University Extension School, and nearly two decades of owning her own production company, she is now engaging her love of design, helping others, and business by owning her own company Janet Roche Designs, LLC. Her company believes that they can find real design solutions to the human condition.

In 2019, Janet launched her own podcast, Inclusive Designers™, and in 2020 started Trauma Informed Design Society, along J. Davis Harte and Christine Cowart. Janet and Christine do a variety of presentations on trauma-informed care and Trauma-informed Design for marginalized populations and consult on projects around the world.

ADRIENNE ERDMAN, MDS

With a background in human factors engineering and consulting, Adrienne has over 10 years of experience as an applied researcher and workshop facilitator who collaborates with architects, designers, and invested parties to create innovative evidence-based and human-centered designs. Versed in various methods, she conducts studies and leverages data to uncover needs, identify design solutions fit for purpose, and assess design effectiveness and efficiency.

J. DAVIS HARTE, PHD, WELL AP

Davis Harte is a leader in health and wellbeing design. She is the Director and Faculty of the Design for Human Health masters program at the Boston Architectural College. She is a WELL Accredited Professional (WELL AP) – a health and well-being credential that denotes expertise in the WELL Building Standard.

Davis is an educator, advocate, practitioner, and speaker who bridges trauma-inform designed spaces, children's places, and also birth environments with brain, neuroscientific and environmental psychological knowledge. She holds a PhD in Health from the University of Technology Sydney, where she penned "The Childbirth Supporter Study: Video-ethnographic examination of the physical birth unit environment." Davis is a co-founder of both the Global Birth Environment Design Network and the Trauma-informed Design Society.

www.ingramcontent.com/pod-product-compliance
Lightning Source LLC
Chambersburg PA
CBHW040844120626
46547CB00001B/19